HENDRIK M. RUITENBEEK was born in 1928 in Leiden, Holland. A distinguished scholar and psychotherapist, he was awarded a doctorate in sociology and law from the University of Leiden, following which he received extensive psychological and psychoanalytic training in the United States and abroad. Dr. Ruitenbeek has subsequently taught at various colleges. At present he is practicing psychoanalysis in New York City, and is also on the faculty of the American Institute for Psychotherapy and Psychoanalysis. He is the editor or author of several books, among which are *PSYCHOANALYSIS AND CONTEMPORARY AMERICAN CULTURE, VARIETIES OF PERSONALITY THEORY, VARIETIES OF MODERN SOCIAL THEORY, THE INDIVIDUAL AND THE CROWD, PSYCHOANALYSIS AND EXISTENTIAL PHILOSOPHY, FREUD AND AMERICA* and *THE MALE MYTH.*

THE NEW GROUP THERAPIES

Dr. Hendrik Ruitenbeek

DISCUS BOOKS/PUBLISHED BY AVON

AVON BOOKS
A division of
The Hearst Corporation
959 Eighth Avenue
New York, New York 10019

First Discus Edition, November, 1970
Third Printing, September, 1972

DISCUS BOOKS TRADEMARK REG. U.S. PAT. OFF. AND
FOREIGN COUNTRIES, REGISTERED TRADEMARK—
MARCA REGISTRADA, HECHO EN CHICAGO, U.S.A.

Printed in the U.S.A.

for Dr. Richard McConchie

de dag is nieuw de dag is oud
de duinen veraderen van positie
en wij drijven als wolken over
het land dalend en stijgend naar
nimmer ontdekte groene bossen

Hans Lodeizen

"For our own past is covered by the
currents of action,
But the torments of others remain an
experience
Unqualified, unworn by subsequent at-
trition.
People change, and smile: but the
agony abides."

T. S. Eliot, *Four Quartets*

"a journey to the center of self"

a group member

"*We* ourselves are the veil."

Ronald Laing

CONTENTS

PREFACE

This is a critical book about the many new group therapies, which have been presented to us in the last decade. I have attempted to give credit there where credit is due, but also have expressed many of my personal doubts on the various new groups. I believe in group therapy and in honesty and openness in the therapeutic process, but I also believe that we should not reject in psychotherapy the many insights we have gained.

I owe many friends and colleagues thanks for advice, wise counsel, unpublished papers, occasional hints, and chance meetings which all contributed to this book. I owe my patients thanks, those in group and outside, who told me about their experiences with some of the new groups. Psychoanalysts are supposedly to be listeners, but I also have argued with friends, patients and colleagues about the new trends in the field of group therapy.

In the end I want to thank especially Dr. Richard McConchie for his unfailing support in the writing of this book.

DR. HENDRIK M. RUITENBEEK

New York
Tangiers

INTRODUCTION

There was a time when traditional psychotherapy was even reluctant to recognize group psychotherapy as a valid adjunct to individual psychotherapy. The book that the reader is about to read should be solid testimony to the fact that not only has group therapy become a recognized and respected branch of psychotherapy, but, at least in the United States, is surpassing individual psychotherapy both in dynamic growth and in the unlimited possibilities it offers to the contemporary patient.

The origins of what one now calls traditional group psychotherapy are somewhat confusing. Early group psychotherapy was completely empirical. One of the early attempts at group psychotherapy were the tuberculosis classes of Dr. Joseph Pratt, which he started in Boston in the early 1900s. Tuberculosis was both a social and a physical disease during that time, and Pratt's patients were discouraged and disheartened. In the spring of 1905 he "formulated a plan for the treatment of consumption in the homes of poor patients. The organization was called a tuberculosis class . . ."[1] These classes were conducted by Pratt

[1]See J. H. Pratt, "The Tuberculosis Class: An Experiment in Home Treatment," *Proceedings, N.Y. Conference, Hosp. Soc. Serv.*, 4 (1917), pp. 49-68. See also another report by Pratt in my book *Group Therapy Today: Styles, Methods, and Techniques* (New York: Atherton Press, 1969), p. 9.

and he supplied in fact his patients with supportive therapy.

The origins of group psychotherapy naturally date back much further than the tuberculosis classes of Dr. Pratt. Since the essence of group psychotherapy is the sharing and interaction of people sometimes with common themes there seems to be little doubt that a lot of this was found in the Greek drama, many medieval plays and in the rather bourgeois nineteenth century discussion societies and clubs, which were so prevalent in Europe at that time. In this chapter I would like to deal briefly with the formal history of group psychotherapy. In chapter 1 we will discuss more in detail the sociological roots of group psychotherapy. Suffice to say, first of all, that the great master of psychoanalysis, Sigmund Freud, had little to do with the growth of group psychotherapy. Ernest Jones relates[2] that probably the first group therapy session was held on board the ship that took Freud, Jung and Ferenczi to America in 1909, where Freud was to receive a honorary doctorate from Clark University. He (Jones) tells us that the three men shared their dreams at breakfast and discussed their feelings and interpretations of these dreams, but there are indications of earlier attempts at group psychotherapy, certainly before 1909, so we should not attribute too much importance to Jones' observation other than its being a nice anecdote.

Returning to Pratt, it is evident from his early writings that he had little understanding of what he was doing in his weekly groups. Later on he became somewhat more sophisticated. Pratt himself attributed some influence on his work to the French

---

[2]See Ernest Jones, *The Life and Work of Sigmund Freud,* Vol. II, p. 55.

physician Joseph Jules Dejerine, who had done some significant work in the treatment of psychoneurosis.[3] Dejerine worked with methods of emotional reeducation and had been doing so for about fifteen years. Pratt followed Dejerine's essential concepts in his later group therapy techniques, citing Dejerine's statement, "Psychotherapy depends wholly and exclusively upon the beneficial influence of one person on another. . . ."[4]

It is interesting to note that before World War I there were several physicians in the United States who began independently to use group psychotherapy approaches with their patients. In an article, published in 1921, E. W. Lazell described his group psychotherapy with schizophrenics:[5]

> The advantages of the group method are many; the success is assured by the results obtained. (1) The patient is socialized with reference to the fear of death and the sexual problem, and feels that since there are so many others in the same condition as himself he cannot be so bad. (2) The fear of the analyst as an individual is removed. (3) It was found that many patients apparently absolutely inaccessible heard and retained much of the material even though they sat and phantasied or talked to themselves all the time the lecture was in progress.

---

[3]See J. H. Pratt, "The Use of Dejerine's Methods in the Treatment of Common Neuroses by Group Psychotherapy," Bull, New England Medical Center, XV (1953), pp. 1-9.

[4]J. Dejerine and E. Gauckler, *The Psychoneuroses and Their Treatment* (Philadelphia: J. B. Lippincott, 1913).

[5]E. W. Lazell, "The Group Treatment of Dementia Praecox," *The Psychoanalytic Review*, 8 (1921), pp. 168–179.

Lazell's group therapy consisted mainly of presenting lectures to his patients in a group, there was thus little interaction. Around 1930 the American psychiatrist and former minister L. Cody Marsh published an article about his group work with psychotics.[6] Marsh employed a religious revival technique, which apparently was very inspirational and somewhat effective. He employed also such techniques as formal lectures, art classes and dance classes.* One of the underlying notions in Marsh's work was that patients in the group should be supportive of one another.

One of the other early American group practitioners on the scene was Trigant Burrow. He used the term group analysis as early as in 1925.[7] Burrow was one of the early and most noteworthy founders of psychoanalysis proper in the United States.[8] Before 1920 he already had made significant contributions to psychoanalysis. Brill introduced Burrow to Freud when the latter visited the United States in 1909. He also met Jung at the same time and elected to study under Jung in Zurich. Why Burrow chose Jung rather than Freud remains somewhat unclear. On the other hand, in 1909 Freud and Jung were still very close and there was at least at that time no sign of an impending crisis between the two. He studied

---

[6]L. C. Marsh, "Group Treatment by the Psychological Equivalent of the Revival," *Mental Hygiene*, 15 (1931), pp. 328–349.

*It seems interesting to note here that in the early days of group psychotherapy the therapists were less structured in their approaches to the group and in effect experimented quite a bit.

[7]Trigant Burrow, "The Group Method of Analysis," *The Psychoanalytic Review*, 14 (1927), pp. 268–280.

[8]See my book *Freud and America* (New York: Macmillan, 1966), in which I describe in detail Burrow's early role in the American psychoanalytic Association.

with Jung in 1910 and after he returned in 1910 he became one of the founding members of the American Psychoanalytic Association. He planned to have some additional analysis with Freud in 1913 but the outbreak of World War I prevented him from doing so. Since 1912 Burrow had become dissatisfied with the emphasis psychoanalysis placed on the individual, an emphasis he felt excluded social forces. He felt strongly that behavioral disorders should be traced back to social relatedness and that research should be carried out in a group setting. Together with Clarence Shileds he developed a method of group psychoanalysis, which he later called phyloanalysis and which stated simply that man is part of a group and that the analysis of the individual can never be completed without real study of the group of which he is an essential part. Freud disagreed with the notions of Burrow and eventually Burrow moved away from the psychoanalytic community. He later complained bitterly that his contributions to the later work of Harry Stack Sullivan were not acknowledged.[9]

Rudolph Dreikurs has pointed out[10] that Alfred Adler, one of the early associates of Freud, became interested in organizing working-class groups and established guidance centers (in Vienna) that used group concepts in treating patients. Dreikurs maintained that German, Austrian, Russian and Danish psychotherapists were using group methods before 1930.

As we shall discuss later, it is relevant to note here that group psychotherapy has relationship to the par-

---

[9]See *A Search for Man's Sanity: The Selected Letters of Trigant Burrow* (New York: Oxford University Press, 1958).

[10]Rudolph Dreikurs, "Early Experiments with Group Psychotherapy," *American Journal of Psychotherapy*, 13 (1959), pp. 219–255.

ticular culture in which it is being practiced. The United States was apparently very receptive to new techniques. Psychoanalysis stemmed from an environment of the intellectual and financial elite in Vienna. Adler was also a socialist and very much interested in the problems of the working class. It was because of this interest that he attempted to adapt the techniques of individual psychotherapy so that large groups of people could be reached. In the clinics he founded, the services of educators and social workers were used.

It is the claim of Jacob Moreno that he used group therapy as far back as 1910,[11] and he also maintains to have coined the term in 1931. Moreno came to the United States in 1925 and before then had been actively using group concepts in Vienna. By 1929 he was publicly demonstrating his methods, and in 1932 his techniques were discussed at a meeting of the American Psychiatric Association.

It seems relevant in the context of this book, which deals with encounter therapy, to discuss some of Moreno's influences in the area of encounter therapy. Paul Johnson described the efforts of Moreno:[12]

> In the spring of 1912 Moreno published in Vienna the first of a series of poetic writings entitled "*Einladung zu einer Begegnung*" (Invitation to an Encounter), which is evidently the first literary definition of encounter, the concept which has become central in the existentialist movement. To describe the encounter, he portrays two persons exchanging eyes to comprehend and know each

---

[11]See Jacob L. Moreno, *Die Gottheit als Komediant* (Vienna: Anzengruber Verlag, 1911).

[12]Paul Johnson, *Psychology of Religion* (New York: Abingdon Press, 1959), pp. 42–43.

other: "A meeting of two: eye to eye, face to face. And when you are near I will tear your eyes out and place them instead of mine, and you will tear my eyes out and will place them instead of yours, then I will look at you with your eyes and you will look at me with mine." The literary magazine *Daimon*, of which he (Moreno) was the editor, carried in the February issue, 1918, a dramatic dialogue by Moreno entitled "Einladung zu einer Begegnung: Die Gottheit als Autor" (Invitation to an Encounter: The Deity as Author). In this article appears the term "interpersonal communication" (zwischenmenschlicher Verkehr). The term "interpersonal relations," which Robert MacDougall used in 1912, came to prominence in his book *Who Shall Survive* (1934) and in the journal he founded in 1937, *Sociometry: A Journal of Interpersonal Relations.* During the years 1918–1920, Martin Buber was a contributing editor of *Daimon*, and his articles appeared side by side with Moreno's, prophetic of the role each would have in the history of interpersonal theory. The I-Thou concept of God was the keystone of the interpersonal arch as documented in their publications, 1920–23.

Moreno in his own article on the Viennese origins of the encounter movement[13] feels that his concept of encounter as developed above, as early as 1914, was the forerunner of Austrian existentialism, but also of the creative movement of group psychotherapy and psychodrama. As he states, "The meaning

[13] J. L. Moreno, "The Viennese Origins of the Encounter Movement, Paving the Way For Existentialism, Group Psychotherapy and Psychodrama," *Group Psychotherapy*, Vol. XXII, (1969), pp. 7–16.

of the encounter definition indicates confrontation, a positive correlation between encounter and sensitivity; sociometry, psychodrama and group psychotherapy have served as instruments to facilitate them."

In Moreno's early writings one traces already an awareness of the sensitivity concept, where he writes, for example:

> "There are actors who are connected with one another by an invisible correspondence of feelings, who have a sort of heightened sensitivity for their mutual inner processes, one gesture is sufficient and often they do not look at one another, they communicate through a new sense as if by a 'medial understanding.'"[14]

There is also a link between the psychodrama of Moreno and the type of sensitivity training which already took place in 1946 at the Bethel Laboratories in Maine. Gottschalk and Pattison point to that in their overview article on T-groups:[15]

> The direct development of the training laboratory came from the collaboration of three men: Leland Bradford, Ronald Lippitt and Kenneth Benne. All three had an educational background in psychology, experience in working with community educational projects, and involvements in numerous national projects dealing with major social problems related to human relations. They had been

---

[14]J. L. Moreno, *The Theater of Spontaneity* (Boston: Beacon House, 1947), p. 68.

[15]Louis Gottschalk and E. Mansell Pattison, "Psychiatric Perspectives on T-Groups and the Laboratory Movement: An Overview," *The American Journal of Psychiatry*, 126: 6 (December 1969), pp. 823–39.

> exposed to and influenced by J. L. Moreno's methods of psychodrama and had experimented with various role-playing procedures in community educational projects directed toward effecting social change.

It should also be noted here that the Bethel leaders published their early findings between 1938 and 1955 in the journals of the Moreno Institute: *Sociometry* and *Group Psychotherapy*. Kenneth Benne himself acknowledged in his book *Human Relations in Christian Change* this debt to Moreno.

Moreno himself feels that group psychotherapy and psychodrama found its origins in Vienna and cites the gardens of Vienna as one of the original spots where group psychotherapy started.

> My most important beginning was however in the gardens of Vienna. After the regular hours in the public schools, the children gathered daily. There classes were held. They consisted of small groups of from fifteen to twenty children, each under a leader chosen by the children themselves. The forming principle of the class was an Impromptu Test which ascertained the creative denominator of the child. Age differences were minimized. Children of four and ten were frequently found in the same group. The general aim of the classes was on one hand to train the whole organism of the child and not merely one of its functions; on the other hand, to lead them into the experience of "wholes." For example, in the botany class, the child was brought into active contact with the thing-in-itself, a direct response to a direct contact was desired. The child experienced

> the *Tree*. This tree became a center of attention: about the tree the child's imagination and fantasy were let loose. The child learned to love the tree before he analyzed it. Our traditional schools reverse this order. One of the outstanding or happenings in the gardens was the choice of parents. Hundreds of children and hundreds of parents gathered to settle their relationships on a more cosmic level than heretofore. This was done by a play in which the children had an opportunity to reject their present parents and choose new ones. After the choice process had been carried out, each child returned with their new parents.[16]

Indeed the link to *Begegnung* or Encounter is most interesting here since Moreno is usually only identified with psychodrama. Psychodrama is defined as "the science which explores truth by dramatic methods. The method of psychodrama uses mainly five instruments—the stage, the subject or patient, the director, the staff of therapeutic aides or what they call auxiliary egos, and the audience." The stage presents the patient with the opportunity to express himself freely and to be himself. The director serves as a kind of producer, and therapist. He must keep the actor in rapport with the audience, relate to the patient, and interpret. The auxiliary egos are extensions of the director, portraying the imagined or real persons in the patient's life drama. The audience finally is a sounding board of public opinion and may well see one of its own collective problems portrayed on the stage.

---

[16] J. L. Moreno, "The Viennese Origins of the Encounter Movement, Paving the Way for Existentialism, Group Psychotherapy and Psychodrama," *Group Psychotherapy*, Vol. XXII, (1969), nos. 1, 2, p. 13.

Other American analysts who experimented with group therapy in the early thirties were Louis K. Wender and Paul Schilder. Wender practiced mainly group psychotherapy with borderline patients in a mental hospital setting. He published his findings in 1935.[17] He considered his work as primarily psychoanalytic and did not care too much for educational and orientative techniques. He also felt that group psychotherapy was applicable only to disorders in which some degree of affect was present and in which intellectual impairment was absent. The groups he conducted consisted of six to eight patients of the same sex who met two or three times each week for one-hour sessions. He encouraged combined treatment, the patient being seen both for individual treatment and in the group setting. He felt that the group represented the family of the patient with the therapist as the symbolic parent and the other patients as siblings.

In 1934 Paul Schilder, who was for many years a close follower of Freud, utilized psychoanalytic concepts in an experiment in group psychotherapy. He described his work with fifty patients in the outpatient department of the psychiatric division of Bellevue Hospital in New York City, when he reported the study at the annual meeting of the American Psychiatric Association in 1936.[18] It stands to reason that Schilder probably was influenced by Freud's theoretical paper on group psychology.[19]

---

[17]Louis Wender, "The Dynamics of Group Psychotherapy and Its Application," *Journal of Nervous & Mental Diseases,* 84 (1936), pp. 54–60.

[18]Paul Schilder, "Results and Problems of Group Psychotherapy in Severe Neurosis," *Mental Hygiene,* 23 (1939), pp. 87–98.

[19]Sigmund Freud, *Group Psychology and the Analysis of the Ego, Standard Edition,* XVIII, p. 67.

One of the pioneers in the early thirties in America undoubtedly was Samuel Slavson, who worked with activity group psychotherapy at the Jewish Board of Guardians. His concepts were a blend of group work, progressive education and psychoanalysis. Activity group therapy emphasizes the acting out of conflicts, impulses, and behavior patterns in group setting. The therapist is permissive and accepting in the group setting as the patients interact with one another. Slavson applied this approach mainly to the treatment of children up to the age of fifteen.

The end of World War II marked the real beginnings of group psychotherapy. First of all there were reports of considerable and important group psychotherapy being done in England. Joshua Bierer organized social club groups among patients, using Adlerian concepts as a theory base for his work.[20] S. H. Foulkes, another English pioneer in group therapy,[21] employed psychoanalytic techniques for his groups but developed his own group psychotherapy theory. He rejects two hypotheses, the first being the Freudian concept of Eros and Thanatos, the second, that an independent social drive leads to the behavior observed in the group. In his opinion the group is a more fundamental unit than the individual. Foulkes is very close in his thinking to Gestalt psychology, and as such there are interesting links between him and the Gestalt therapists.

An even more interesting link with the new encounter techniques exists in the work of the English group therapist W. R. Bion, who has set forth a series

---

[20]J. Bierer, ed., *Therapeutic Social Clubs* (London: H. K. Lewis, 1948).

[21]S. H. Foulkes and E. J. Anthony, *Group Psychotherapy* (London: Penguin Books, 1957).

of rather complex hypotheses concerning the processes he believes to be present in all groups. The processes are set up as conscious and rational as well as emotional and irrational.[22]

He developed the theory that a group can be described as a series of emotional states or basic assumption cultures. Affective need was deeply tied in with the work the group was attempting. As the individuals in the group reacted against the cultures or agreed to accept the cultures, they would contribute to the work of the group. According to Bion the relationship between the individual and the group culture was grouped under a series of "valences." The individual is moving along the valence of pairing, dependency, or "fight-flight." The process of group movement can be seen in a series of shifts from one emotional culture to another, based on the valence. Thus, at all times, the leader is able to ask, "What is the group really doing at this moment? Is it attempting to avoid, or to get to, a problem?" This would be the emotional culture. Bion provided the group with no direction or structure, and the patients' reactions to the lack of structure—his anger or confusion—was the material initially used for exploration. Indeed this comes very close to the situations that arise in the current encounter groups, where structure or direction is ignored and where the material is produced right there and interpreted on the spot.

A last pioneer of group psychotherapy in the United States to be mentioned is certainly Alexander Wolf, whose article on the psychoanalysis of groups

---

[22]W. R. Bion, "Group Dynamics: A Review," *The International Journal of Psycho-Analysis,* 33 (1952), pp. 235–47.

became a classic in the field.[23] He conducts fairly traditional groups. He was influenced by Louis Wender and Paul Schilder, and by 1940 he was working with five groups of eight to ten patients each. Wolf applies the principles of individual psychoanalysis to the group setting, using major tools of the psychoanalytic method: transference, dreams, life-history taking and free association.

Regardless of claims made by various people as their being the inventors of group psychotherapy, it seems obvious that no great mind was the originator of group psychotherapy. That in itself might have contributed to a far less rigid context in which group psychotherapy was conceived and developed. Individual psychoanalysis is still tied to the heritage of Sigmund Freud, and in many instances justifiably so. A great deal of techniques and styles of work in psychoanalysis are a part of Freud's work and inventive spirit, but at the same time it also, at least for a long time, prevented individual psychoanalysis to come into its own. Too many new techniques were being dismissed as fraudulent and those who tried nevertheless were dismissed as heretics. That the situation for new ways in individual psychoanalysis has improved in the last decades has less to do with a changing attitude of orthodox psychoanalysts but much more with the changing sociological picture of both patient and society. Especially in a dynamic and pragmatic society as the United States, modes of orthodoxy do not last long or at least they are questioned. The rise of neo-Freudian and existential therapy and other forms of new therapies is evidence

---

[23]Alexander Wolf, "The Psychoanalysis of Groups," *American Journal of Psychotherapy*, 3 (1949), pp. 16–50 and No. 4 (1950), pp. 525–58. It is also reprinted in my book *Group Psychotherapy Today* (New York: Atherton Press, 1969).

of the fact that major changes in the individual therapies are occurring right now.[24]

Again such a situation does not and did not exist for group therapy. As a matter of fact there was never too much orthodoxy in early group psychotherapy since group psychotherapy itself was new, inventive and bold.

It might also be interesting to note that the major breakthrough in psychoanalysis is not occurring in individual psychoanalysis but in group psychotherapy. Experimentation within the confines of traditional psychoanalysis always has been difficult, but group psychotherapy already provided the kind of right framework for experimentation. After all if groups meet every week for one hour and a half, why not for three hours? Or for that matter why stop at three and do it a whole weekend, as is being done in the marathons? Such flexibility does not exist in individual psychoanalysis where the time limit of fifty minutes puts natural restraints upon the inventive analyst.

However one thing became clear in the last decade: Individual psychoanalysis alone and even in combination with established group psychotherapy was not any more meeting the demands of our patients. Not that the new and prospective patients necessarily demanded a shortcut to mental health, but they felt that at least in individual psychoanalysis alone they could not communicate the kind of thing that was bothering them. They felt isolated and even alienated in the individual sessions and were at a loss as to how to communicate this to their analysts. Even in existential analysis where there is an emphasis

---

[24]See my book, *A Primer of the New Therapies* (New York: in press, 1971).

upon communication and closeness (sharing) the limits of the traditional psychoanalytic context were being felt.

In mentioning existential analysis we should pause for a moment and discuss some of the implications of existential psychoanalysis in the light of current developments in group psychotherapy. It is one of the amazing stories in the history of psychoanalysis that Freud never broke with the father of existential psychoanalysis: Ludwig Binswanger. To illustrate this one should read the letter that Freud wrote to Binswanger thanking him for a paper Binswanger read at the occasion of Freud's eightieth birthday and where Freud writes:[25]

> As I read it I was delighted with your beautiful language, your erudition, the vastness of your horizon, your tactfulness in contradicting me. As is well known, one can put up with vast quantities of praise . . . *Naturally, for all that, you have failed to convince me* (Binswanger's italics). I have always confined myself to the ground floor and basement of the edifice. You maintain that by changing one's point of view, one can also see the upper story, in which dwell such distinguished guests as religion, art, etc. . . . But probably we are speaking at cross purposes, and our differences will be ironed out only after centuries.

In many ways existential analysis as it was developed by Binswanger, Boss, Merleau-Ponty, and in America by Rollo May, has served to bridge the gap between orthodox analysis and the crisis of man in

---

[25]Ludwig Binswanger, *Sigmund Freud: Reminiscences of a Friendship* (New York, Grune & Stratton, 1957), p. 99.

Western society at mid-century. Not even the post- and neo-Freudians have reached the core of the existential experience of the alienated individual among us. Binswanger clarified for us the situation of our *Eigenwelt* (the world of the self and the person's relation to that self) and while the neo-Freudians, such as Erich Fromm, might have dealt effectively with the concept of the *Mitwelt* (the social world) it was left to the existential analysts to recognize in their patients the despair, alienation, the ontological insecurity (as Laing has called it) and the deeper identity crisis which has beset us in the latter part of this century.

Thus Freud might have sensed that indeed Binswanger was not rejecting Freudian theory, but merely extending the psychoanalytic potential, whereby a subtle shift occurred from the analysis of the psyche to the analysis of *Dasein* (or Being). Where in the encounter therapies we recognize the desire of the patient to be himself, a person, who can choose and decide for himself and for himself alone, we should credit existential analysis with paving the way. Binswanger formulated it in the following words when he talks of existential analysis vis-à-vis the patient and states that existential analysis tries to understand the patient's life history, but it does "not explain this life history and its pathologic idiosyncrasies according to the teaching of any school of psychotherapy, or by means of its preferred categories. *Instead,* it understands this life history as modifications of the total structure of the patient's being-in-the-world . . ."[26]

What we see today in the encounter groups in

[26]Ludwig Binswanger, "Existential Analysis and Psychotherapy," Hendrik M. Ruitenbeek, ed., *Psychoanalysis and Existential Philosophy* (New York, E. P. Dutton, 1962), p. 19.

terms of directness, honesty and openness, we certainly can trace back to some of the work done by the existential group therapists. Thomas Hora, in formulating some of the elements of existential group therapy puts it this way: "Authentic group participation—that is, genuine being-in-the-group—is only possible under conditions of *openness, receptivity,* and *responsiveness* toward the world."[27]

It is most probable that the rapid rise of *all* forms of group psychotherapy is due to the fact that individual psychotherapy by and large has not been able to cope with the particular kind of new patient who has presented himself on the doorstep of many psychotherapists in the last decade or two. It is perhaps that the American character per se, as we will discuss in a later chapter in more detail, is a breeding ground for the kind of isolated and alienated (lonely, if you will) individual. Those types of patients are vague in their complaints about themselves and others, although they verbalize rather well; there is an air of discontent about them, a general malcontent with the way things are, they have little to fall back upon, their childhood memories are not necessarily traumatic or even very bad, but there is not too much they feel good about. They do function pretty well in their jobs and in the world at large, but they lack the touch of intimacy and warmth, which are the ingredients for plain happiness and satisfaction. There is something mechanistic about them all and it is perhaps a general trend in our culture today which we are talking about. Rollo May wrote not too long ago about this and said, "There is plenty of evidence that the sense of isolation, the alienation of one's self from

---

[27]Thomas Hora, "Existential Psychiatry and Group Psychotherapy," Hendrik M. Ruitenbeek (ed.), *Psychoanalysis and Existential Philosophy* (New York: E. P. Dutton, 1962), p. 132.

the world is suffered not only by people in pathological condition, but by countless 'normal' persons as well in our day." So in a sense it is obvious that individual psychotherapy was somewhat at a loss as to how to deal with this type of patient. The new patient did not fit any of the classic schemes. Sure, these patients are all too willing to talk about themselves, their past and . . . their parents, but does it help? Since we are dealing here with problems which are mainly societal and stemming from the rapidly changing face of our contemporary society, it becomes clear that the tools of individual psychoanalytic therapy are not at all sufficient or workable in that kind of situation. One can make some generalizations about such new patients. They are by and large rather *passive* in their interaction with others. As a matter of fact the whole idea of *assertion* is somewhat alien to them. There is part of them which prefers vastly to be told what to do rather than find out for themselves and *decide*. It is somewhat amazing to find out in talking to these patients that the idea of confrontation and decision-making in their personal lives is something which is alien to them. The appeal of existential therapy with its stress on confrontation and choice (i.e., decision) points to a need in these patients which is not being met by the society in which they live.

All the new group therapies, discussed in this book, do resemble one another in fundamental principle: that the established individual and group therapies simply are not working any more for a significant number of patients. It might be good to realize that the new group therapies do not necessarily reject the established therapies, and why should they? I am sure that a great number of my colleagues experience the same thing as I have in my practice, i.e., what works for one patient does not necessarily work for the other. I also am sure that many therapists in their individual practice and in their group experience already have quietly applied perhaps rather unorthodox methods and techniques without rushing them out for publication in the established journals. My friend Masud Khan elsewhere has pointed to this fact, where he writes: "We analysts seem to have a poor tolerance of each other's style and sensibility of clinical handling of the patient. We tend to *hide* or understate the truly personal *creative* ventures in our clinical work, because we fear that to seek help through a candid discussion would provoke only envy or carping criticism from our colleagues."[28] The flood of new group therapies is in my opinion also the result of the quiet work of many therapists around the country, who were convinced that somehow a lot of the old techniques and methods in their practice simply did not work with a considerable number of patients. We all have in our various experiences with patients come to a point where we felt that perhaps some of the old taboos in psychoanalysis did not make too much sense to us any more.[29]

The taboos in psychoanalysis have to a great extent inhibited many patients who simply could not work through or work with the rules of established psychoanalysis. Not too much attention has been given in the literature of psychoanalysis to the failures of psychoanalysis and psychoanalysts with patients who

---

[28]M. Masud R. Khan, "On Symbiotic Omnipotence," *The Psychoanalytic Forum*, John A. Lindon, ed. Science House, 1969.

[29]I want to refer the reader to an excellent paper by Dr. Elizabeth Mintz on "Touch and the Psychoanalytic Tradition" (to be published), where she in great detail discusses one of the major taboos of orthodox psychoanalysis—touch.

were not ready to work within the established framework or context of psychoanalysis. The absence of such papers on failure is perhaps due to an attitude of many psychoanalysts in refusing to come to terms with such failures or perhaps simply denying them. What I am saying is that again much of what has come out in the new group psychotherapies and individual therapies has to do with a lack of insight (and foresight) on the part of many analysts of the present and past. Too often we get the impression that the psychoanalytic establishment is only reading and absorbing their own papers asd thoughts. There is fatal inbreeding in the psychoanalytic establishment which prevents creative thinking and new and bold steps in the process of both individual and group therapy.

Too many analysts still consider the appearance of new techniques and methods in the psychoanalytic process as a threat to their own established way of thinking, thereby ignoring the fact that psychotherapy like everything is a *continuum*, a process of growth and development. Ignoring this is fatal both to the patient and the analyst.

The new group therapies have such an appeal to the contemporary patient because they offer him new and unorthodox ways of dealing with his problems. Sociologically it is even more understandable that the new group therapies hit such fertile ground, since most people feel hemmed in and closed up by the conventional processes of society. But how can they escape? Sociologists have been saying for a few decades that in an other-directed society like ours it seems quite difficult for the individual to assert any kind of autonomy for himself, hence the general sense of helplessness and almost deadening feeling of fate, which brought all of this upon us. Even the most outstanding contemporary social scientists agree that the alternatives to the harnessed structure of the other-directed, technological culture are few and far between.*

It should be noted that there are still a considerable number of inner-directed Americans left, but the appeal of the new group therapies undoubtedly is to be found among the suburban middle class who are not inner-directed. As a matter of fact I would even venture to say that individual therapy as a learning and educational process is probably more appealing to the inner-directed individual rather than the group-oriented approach which appeals to the other-directed man.

So many people fall in between the structure which they really do not like or desire and the alternative which is in many cases unattainable. It is precisely that kind of a situation which puts many people into trouble or trouble spots. They start to flounder in their personal lives and often also in their business or professional areas. So they are seeking help and advice. Individual orthodox psychotherapy does not hold too many promises for them since they feel that again they are trapped in a structured situation. Group therapy and especially the new and advanced experimental group therapies offer them many more opportunities to express themselves, to confront others, and to share some of the concerns about life and society, sex and love, home and profession with others of a like mind and similar problems.

We have arrived at a situation in psychotherapy where we simply had to create a broader context for

*David Riesman has discussed some alternatives in the last chapter on autonomy in his book, *The Lonely Crowd*. I have mentioned some sketchy alternatives in my books, *The Individual and The Crowd* and *The Male Myth*.

the neurotic of *our* time. Many of the clichés of the past simply do not work any more. Moreover, they do not work any more *both* for patient *and* for therapist. In a group-oriented society such as America it was understandable that new inventions in psychotherapy would be most progressive and successful in the field of group psychotherapy. Americans by and large always have felt more comfortable in groups,* and are also less concerned about their privacy or the lack thereof than Europeans. There seems to be a ready eagerness on the part of many Americans to talk about their most intimate problems with anyone who is available at the time. Groups therefore are no obstacle to them; on the contrary the group stimulates them to express whatever is bothering them at the time.† In our chapter on the American character and group therapy we will look at some more material along this line.

Another reason for the appeal of the new group therapies is also probably the kind of openness with which many Americans greet new developments in every field. The orthodoxy which one encounters in individual therapy is by and large still due to the influx and influence of the German-Austrian orthodox therapists.

There are some other aspects to the emergence of the new "turned-on" groups. The message given to all seekers (mainly middle class) who attend Esalen, gurus, massage centers, marathons, encounter groups,

---

*That marvelous and perceptive observer of the American scene, Alexis de Tocqueville, already noticed this in his book *Democracy in America.*

†I have had several foreign observer-analysts sit in on my groups, and they all were amazed at the total lack of inhibition with which the group members discussed their problems. Moreover they commented about a certain style and smoothness which they found outstanding in their observation.

"feel" groups, "movement" groups, truth laboratories, and the like, is that they should live in the now. If one is leading a successful, firmly structured life, it is easy to dismiss (as many observers do) such vague messages as silly. But for many people the need to replace the waning authoritarianism and otherness of religion with some positive form of self-containment is very real. The Ouspensky groups in England used to do much the same thing—and probably still do.

One of the sad aspects of some of the new groups is that some people seem to have to destroy so much—particularly in the games-playing truth groups—before they can attain any kind of peace. And often the jargon of psychoanalysis is replaced with the jargon of the "hip" seeking, searching, but often clever and calculated individual, who in turn falls victim to the same kind of dull conformity from which he is trying to escape.

In her book *Turning On,* Rasa Gustaitis maintains that ". . . the science and technology that created the new freedoms also created much more sophisticated methods for potential control over human beings. The biggest question now is who will do the controlling."[30] She feels that people like Frederick Perls (Esalen) and Carl Rogers (client-centered therapy), and others, will have us become more fully our own instruments.

But every man and every movement has its own style and its own insistence upon being right and being heard. There are those who already compare Frederick Perls to Freud and are becoming in fact as dogmatic in their following of Perls as some of Freud's followers. In all of the emerging new group

---

[30]Rasa Gustaitis, *Turning On* (New York: Macmillan, 1969), p. 317.

movements one detects an impatience with what was, but there is also an intolerance of what still *is*. I still maintain that insights into one's own psyche and . . . problems have to be acquired and worked through. Whatever people gain in the new group therapy movements still seems somewhat tentative. The follow-up studies are scarce or nonexistent,* and the papers written on the new groups are often highly subjective and partial.

Closely related to the new group therapies is of course the infatuation with drugs of many who are involved in the new group therapies. After all, LSD and other mind-expanding drugs promised the long-expected shortcut to a more fulfilling and stable life. If I am skeptical about some of the new group therapies, I am even more skeptical about the significance and value—Aldous Huxley notwithstanding—of the mind-expanding drugs in the process of both group and individual psychotherapy. So many laymen and irresponsible professional people have dabbled with drugs and made such nonsensical generalizations about their ultimate value for psychotherapy that we would be better off with concentrating on what we really have in terms of potential and growth.

Another aspect of the new group psychotherapies is that we have not fully decided if they suffice to meet the needs of the patient. In other words, should the patient also be engaged in individual psychotherapy in order to consolidate his insights and growth? Many believe that the new group therapies can do it on their own, that the patient who presents himself to any of the experiences is probably not suitable material for individual psychotherapy to be-

*Psychotherapists by and large often have been reluctant to do follow-up studies of their patients. Hence the amount of speculation about the efficacy of psychotherapy.

gin with. On the other hand a considerable number of therapists take a dim view of stirring up so much emotional content in a patient in the group experience and then simply leave him, or worse, dismiss him with it. In my own experience with marathons I have found it extremely valuable to work in these marathons with my *own* individual patients, whom I had known in individual psychotherapy for a number of years.

All of these hazards, to be sure, will be discussed in more detail once we engage ourselves in this book in a more thorough investigation of some of the new group therapies. The discussion of those hazards does not necessarily mean a rejection on my part of these new group therapies, but they are a part of my attempt to bring all of these new experiences into a proper focus.

It should also be noted, that until quite recently, the process of group psychotherapy was somewhat conventional. The group would convene once a week for one hour and a half, and the eight or nine members (or fewer) would interact in the exchange of their problems and their interpretations of one another's actions and words. Therapists would play a relatively passive role, giving some guidance and some interpretation. Sometimes the group would meet a second time without the therapist, but that would be the extent of the process. There were and even are minor differences in detail, such as the matter of being on first-name terms with the therapist, but on the whole group psychotherapy continued to proceed rather conventionally in the early 1950s.

All this changed in the late 1950s and early 1960s. Work with restricted groups, limited to artists, alcoholics, and persons with similar problems, for example, was introduced. Married couples were included in groups of single people; groups of limited time span as contrasted to the relatively time-consuming open groups became somewhat of a novelty in the field of group psychotherapy.

Innovation did not halt there. The marathon group proved to be one of the first major breakthroughs in the conventional group therapy process. The therapist often acted in this situation by introducing his own personality on a par with the other members of the group. The marathon group became so well known that *The New Yorker* devoted an article to the subject.[31] As far as I know, the first novel on the marathon group was published in 1967 and gave a vivid description of agony and excitement among members of a marathon in California.[32]

In the 1960s the number of novel methods in group psychotherapy has multiplied and has affected the attitudes of many psychotherapists. One of them wrote to me from California and said, "My whole point of view has been shifting recently with some intensive experience with Synanon, and my interest in group-therapy format and technique has been diminishing as my respect for the power of community and simple honesty increases." In California especially, various new forms of group psychotherapy have been introduced.

That does not mean that developments in the East have been slow. In and around New York there has been a tremendous increase in experimentation with new forms of group psychotherapy. True enough in the process, groups have emerged which do not live up to general standards of ethics and

---

[31]Renata Adler, "The Thursday Group," *The New Yorker* (April 15, 1967), p. 55.

[32]Jerry Sohl, *The Lemon Eaters* (New York: Dell, 1968).

responsible group therapy, but then that probably was to be expected in a period where a flood of new experiments emerged. Also there are many (and not always therapists) who want to be on the bandwagon.

Understandably severe criticisms have been leveled against some of the new forms of group psychotherapy and I feel that many of these cirticisms have been justified. Therapists who are involved in the new forms of group psychotherapy would do well to listen more closely to some of these criticisms.

In reaction to an article by Dr. Fred Stoller, one of the pioneers of the marathon in California,[33] Hyman Spotnitz writes, "When people are given the expectation that they will be able to take care of themselves, Dr. Stoller believes that they 'do a remarkable job of doing just that.' " In my experience, this is not necessarily true. To feel exhilarated and renewed is not invariably therapeutic. The dropping of masks and "learning that the masks are not so necessary" disregards the fact that some masks are vitally needed ego defenses. Some patients are unable to build bridges until they have outgrown their need for barriers.

To return to the major question raised by this report: Can an emotional experience such as Dr. Stoller describes, highly concentrated in time and created in a situation with a built-in sense of urgency, produce significant personality change? The simple truth is that we do not know the answer. If periods of excitement in a new situation can free an individual from the effects of past traumatic events,

---

[33]Frederick H. Stoller, "Accelerated Interaction: A Time-Limited Approach Based on the Brief, Intensive Group," *International Journal of Group Psychotherapy* (April, 1969), Vol. XVIII, no. 2, p. 220.

such an approach may have therapeutic potential. It might, for example, help to mitigate or nullify the effects of another type of deeply emotional experience, such as a paralyzing reaction to the death of a loved one. This possibility might bear investigation. But, in my opinion, there is little likelihood that the method described will be recognized as a form of psychotherapy.[34]

This is harsh criticism, to be sure, but it is included here as indication to the reader that the author too has serious doubts about the ultimate efficacy of the new experimental forms of group psychotherapy as they have emerged in the last decade.

In concluding we should state, however, that the new experimental forms of group psychotherapy are somewhere an answer to the increasing alienation of the modern individual from himself and his environment. As Frederick Weiss has written, "While man's outer space is expanding, his inner space is shrinking. As man makes new contact with the universe, he loses contact with his self." Our boundaries have been broadened from an exclusive concern with the insane to include the treatment of neurotics, personality disorders, and those who are afflicted with a host of so-called minor emotional distresses. However we have continued to apply the same label, alienation, to a symptom that we now consider pathognomonic of our time: The final common pathway into which our defensive systems flow. What had been forensic psychiatric terms used to describe the symptoms of the most unfortunate is now applied to all patients regardless of their diagnoses. The symptoms presented today by our patients and by our society have confronted us so directly with the universal and poly-

[34]Discussion by Hyman Spotnitz, *ibid.*, p. 236.

morphous quality of alienation that we cannot deny its overpowering influence in shaping contemporary behavior. From all this stems, in short, many of the new approaches to group psychotherapy; they are an illustration of the increasing discomfort, which is so difficult to verbalize for many patients, of many of our contemporary patients. The methods and techniques of the new forms of group psychotherapy, as described in this book, are very much a part of the turmoil in which the individual finds himself today.

THE ROOTS OF GROUP PSYCHOTHERAPY

It might be important to state at the outset that the roots or origins of group psychotherapy are much different than those of individual psychotherapy. As we have remarked earlier, group psychotherapy existed in disguised forms for quite some time. The need to *share* one's feelings with other people and express in the company of others, was and is for many a therapeutic experience. That need has been met in various forms of human interaction since a long time. And amazingly enough one also notices great similarities between the disguised forms of group psychotherapy of the past and the overt manifestations of group psychotherapy today. What for example is really the difference between the psychodrama syndrome of Moreno and the participation of many an audience in various medieval plays? Such participation undoubtedly was cathartic and provided a way for many to express some of their hidden feelings and desires, which probably could not be expressed in the world at large. Although psychodrama is a *deliberate* attempt to force the participants to act out their feelings and possible life-designs and where of course in the participation of the audience in medieval plays such a deliberate attempt did not exist, nevertheless it provided many with the opportunity to express oneself in a rather unorthodox and safe way.

Of course, one might say that the needs for individual psychotherapy were also met in disguised forms, but the difference with the group psychotherapy forms is that there are few similarities between what individual psychotherapy is today and its forms of the past.

In tracing some of the predecessors of group psychotherapy, and especially where it concerns the most recent expressions of group psychotherapy such as the marathon and the Gestalt experiences (which are all loaded with emotional overtones), one also remembers the religious revival movements in the United States, which provided for many a platform (an emotional platform, that is) for the expression (and often exhibition!) of one's emotional hangups. After all, one should realize that such expressions of emotion and exhibition have to find a way out of the confines of one's own personality, and in the context of time and place it was perfectly legitimate to *use* those religious movements as an emotional vehicle. To be sure this was not recognized by the participants and originators of those movements. On the contrary any suggestion to this effect probably would have horrified them. It is interesting to note that ministers were instrumental in some of the early forms of group psychotherapy in this country. Dr. Elwood Worcester, the rector of the Emmanuel Church in Boston, advanced five hundred dollars to Dr. Pratt to support him in the conduct of his tuberculosis classes. Eventually Dr. Worcester and Dr. Samuel McComb founded the Emmanuel Church health classes, known as the Emmanuel Church Movement. Both these clergymen were in turn helped by one of the first American psychoanalysts, Isadore Coriat. This movement eventually became the focus of a critical editorial in the journal of the New York State Medical Society. The editorial noted:

> The Emmanuel Church Movement in Boston which has resulted in establishing a clinic for the treatment of functional nervous and mental disorders, under the directorship of an able pastor, Dr. Worcester, has assumed such serious proportions and has been widely exploited . . .[1]

The editorial then went on to critisize clergymen who treated nervous and mental disorders.*

An interesting footnote might be that the Emmanuel Church Movement was placed in Boston, which was (and is) also the home of the Christian Science movement. Here too, religious people, in this case laymen (practioners, as they are called), got

---

[1]"The Emmanuel Church Movement in Boston," *New York Med. Journal,* 87 (1908), pp. 1047–48.

*It is interesting to note that clergymen apparently, at least in this country, have been involved in the early origins of psychoanalysis and sociology. It is well known that many of the early pioneers in sociology were trained ministers.

involved in the treatment of physical and mental illness. And those who are familiar with the Christian Science testimonial Wednesday meetings know that a great deal of emotional discharge takes place in that setting with either positive or negative effect.

In all of this we should realize that modern group psychotherapy has *specific* therapeutic aims, while for many of the revival and religious movements this was only a by-product.

In the history of group psychotherapy we should also state that the obvious idea that the subtle interchanges between human beings engaged in psychotherapy (or group psychotherapy, if you will) *cannot* be reduced to the structural concepts of transference-countertransference has finally caught on even among psychoanalysts. Why this took so long must be a mystery to any honest man who ever sat behind couch or desk. There have always been therapists who were prepared to demonstrate the unique interpersonal aspects of psychotherapy out of their own experience, but somehow their arguments were always beaten down by charges of unorthodoxy. If one were to hazard a guess as to what factors have brought about this change of attitude, one should not omit the importance of the new interest in "encounters," which I will discuss in more detail in this book.

Suffice to say that we are currently witnessing an epidemic of "therapeutic encounters." Such encounters are sought out not only in hospitals and clinics, but also in university credit-courses, in professional schools, in theaters, in new communities and in a variety of so-called institutes. At times the emphasis is on sensitivity training, but at other times, as when people disrobe and discuss their bodies or when they are encouraged to fondle, massage, or touch one another, the emphasis seems, rather, to be on insensitivity training. Epidemics can occur only in a vulnerable population, and the vulnerability in this instance seems to derive from the sense of isolation, disillusionment, and anomie which pervades in a particular way, not the middle and upper classes, but in a broader sense the educated classes. Most notably among the younger intelligentsia there is an intense longing for the intimacy that they have learned to expect as the culmination of identity. This is not to say that the current encounter epidemic is a new phenomenon; and here we again return to the history of group psychotherapy; only the language and some of the format are novel. Writing about Cincinnati in 1832, Frances Trollope described an encounter of the era—the revival:

> When the room is full, the company, of whom a vast majority are always women, are invited, entreated, and coaxed to confess before their brothers and sisters all their thoughts, faults, and follies. These confessions are strange scenes; the more they confess, the more invariably are they encouraged and caressed.

The differences between the revival meeting and marathon group therapy, the Living Theater, a weekend at one of the new institutes such as Esalen, and other forms of therapeutic encounter are largely limited to ideology; otherwise, the quality of human experience is markedly similar.

As a matter of fact the religious revival movement in the United States probably served for many years as a means through which many psychological pressures could be released. The simplicity of the revival phenomenon, its appeal not only to a black community, but also to white rural communities, is probably still very much with us.

One should also see that the contemporary "revival" movement in group psychotherapy cannot be sufficiently explained by attributing it to the fact that psychiatric and psychological healing methods have been grossly and unconscionably oversold—which they have been—and are now considered the birthright of every American citizen. Rather, the historical pattern suggests only that our overly zealous salesmanship has affected the form and not the substance.

In all of this there are some, and Ronald Laing was one of its early spokesmen, who seem willing to permit the "quest for an authentic meeting" to become the guiding principle of the new group therapeutic effort. But is this search for an authentic meeting something new?

Is the desire for intimacy, for relatedness, for care, for affection and understanding, anything that is unusual in the history of mankind? I maintain for once that the fact that we have to structure such needs today in the form of encounter groups, in the form of even traditional group therapy, in the form of nude therapy, in the form of marathons, is an indication that contemporary society has lost the ability to provide its people with the natural qualities that would enable them to find the satisfaction of all their needs in a spontaneous and nonstructured manner.

There are examples abundant in the past of such ways and means whereby the people provided for themselves the affection and closeness that apparently we all need no matter what age or time we are living in. The revival meetings undoubtedly are a very good example of an emotional need being met. I already cited the Greek plays and the participation of the audience in the medieval plays.

I can think of other examples that today might be labeled as group therapy in one way or another.

In the eighteenth and nineteenth centuries the so-called Rederijkerskamers[2] were very popular in Holland. People used to gather during the long and cold winter evenings at some common meeting place in the village or town and some subject of general interest, be it religion, politics or ethics, would be discussed. Sometimes there would be an introduction or short lecture by someone chosen beforehand, but the main object would be a lively and interesting discussion. Out of these meetings friendships would develop. Other ideas in terms of the state of the nation or the town would be developed. In general there was a great deal of what we would call today encounter and interaction. Did these people gather for the specific reason of getting a therapeutic result out of all this? Of course not. The need to come together and exchange views, and meet one another was there and was being met. Contrary to the modern group therapeutic forms there was no overt aim or even an admission that something was wrong with the society they lived in and therefore needed this form of interaction. This is of course not the case with our modern group therapy. There is the admittance that something *is* wrong with us and society, and hence we are here to see what we can do about it for ourselves and perhaps for society at large.

What is interesting in all of this is that of course people have always felt the need to get together in groups and exchange ideas or discuss their or other people's problems, but in our day this need apparent-

---

[2]Rederijkerskamers can be translated as simply discussion groups. The word *rederijker* has also the notion of giving or presenting a lecture. As an afterthought, it might be interesting to note that some of the major political parties in Holland found their origin in these discussion groups. I am sure that such discussion groups existed in other countries at that time.

ly cannot be met anymore through the ordinary channels of society. In other words, the breakdown of communication (and that started well before the onset of modern technology) has forced us to establish new and *artificial* forms of human interaction. Apparently our own resources were not quite enough to meet the demands of the twentieth century. Life became more complicated and one simply could not fall back on the prescribed life-patterns of the past.

There seems to be a general desire for authenticity in all the new and various forms of psychotherapy. But somehow where do we connect the past with the present? Are therapists genuine or are they just the providers of a given and needed service? In fact the issue is perhaps general. How do therapists, trainers, basic encounter leaders, resolve questions posed by their own dramaturgical skills—their charismatic capacities? Does the utilization of these invariably mean that the group leader is a "performer" and, by implication, less authentic (!) than he claims to be? This is a serious question, which our research of the roots of group psychotherapy urges upon us. The use of devices by the new group therapies such as trust exercises, dance movement, mood music, and so on, heightens the theatrical aspects of the group experience. Inevitably its leader must appear as a kind of impresario. What is "real" and what is "phony" under such circumstances becomes especially hard to distinguish for participants.

But perhaps the reasons for the new and experimental forms of group psychotherapy are more complex than we think. Many individuals in our society really do feel hemmed in and lonely. And did they feel that way in the nineteenth century? We are beset by the problems of an impersonal technostructure, a war we cannot seem to get decently out of (and did people care, let us say in 1870, about the French–German war? Or did it really affect them?), and social threats that press upon the jugular of this society. Thanks to mobility and progress, relationships are fragmentary and all kinds of people are asking, "Who cares about me?" Some practitioners of sensitivity training view it as a therapeutic technique ideally suited for such problems. So the confrontation and its affectionate resolution are the main vehicles. Who cares? "We (I?) care!" Is alienation the problem? Perhaps now but certainly not a hundred years ago. But then there is the nagging question that we *really* do not know about those people a hundred years ago! So we arrive now at a situation that "We (the group) will provide 'instant' intimacy!" Beside the question of the dramaturgical leader we must place that of the melodramatic group. Staged conflicts and their resolution can be soul satisfying and cathartic—in the same sense as role play and psychodrama, but the latter are most effective as diagnostic aids and are not usually in themselves means of working through conflicts. Further, and more important, does not the "effectiveness" (that is, the drama) of such group experiences depend in fact upon their nonrepetition and their uniqueness with respect to the participant's daily life?

We are far more concerned with the roots of the newer group psychotherapies, because traditional group psychotherapy is far more than an adjunct of traditional individual therapy.

As a matter of fact it seems that the newer group therapies have less and less in common with traditional group or individual psychotherapy. The unconventionality of most of the new group therapies does not stem from any roots in traditional group therapy.

Traditional group psychotherapy by and large adopted over the years most of the aspects and implications of individual psychotherapy. The dynamics of transference and countertransference, the relatively neutral position of the analyst, the noninvolvement of the group analyst, the type of patients admitted to traditional group phychotherapy (most were neurotic), the traditional techniques of nonintervention and listening, the rather circumscribed pattern of behavior of both therapist and patients in the group—all of that was as much a part and a heritage of individual psychotherapy and simply was adopted by traditional group psychotherapy.

This all has virtually vanished in the new group therapies. Not that there is not transference or countertransference, but the *handling* of these issues by the traditional analyst is far different from the new group therapist, who in fact has all but dismissed the traditional approach to transference and countertransference. I think in terms of the history of the new group therapies it is important to realize this. Perhaps it is true that the new group psychotherapies see their heritage more in the line and history of the desire for human encounter rather than the invention of one person.

The attraction of encounter groups, marathons, play therapy, psychodrama and other forms of group therapy where the patient actually is allowed to participate and even act out some of his desires and aggressions, that attraction it should be said is the greatest and most widespread in the urban centers of contemporary America. I feel that this has a great deal to do with the decline in community life in those centers, if it ever existed in the first place, and with the steady rise in alienation and estrangement of big-city people. The loss of a sense of community and the absence of meaningful social activities probably has contributed to the desire to participate in the groups mentioned above. Often one hears the remark, even in traditional groups which I have conducted for a number of years, that the group activity provides the patient not only with a platform to air his problems but also with the opportunity to establish genuine relationships and encounters. True again this might not have been the prime goal of traditional group therapy but it certainly has become an important by-product of the process.

We have been listening now for years to our sociologists who have told us about the loneliness of the contemporary individual, his inability to establish meaningful friendships and relationships, the absence of goals in his life and a certain dullness that pervades his life. These signs were already there in the late forties and the early fifties, and the remedies or a search for a solution have now become crucial in the sixties and will probably even be more so in the early seventies.

In other words, if no viable solutions are to be found for the lack of communication and community among us, the urge to participate in all kinds of therapeutic group experiences will become stronger.

In looking at the roots of the newer group psychotherapies, one cannot help but ponder the very roots of psychotherapy, and I think there is some validity and a *raison d'être* to make some observations on psychotherapy in general and at the same time linking them to group psychotherapy in general. In making these observations here I am indebted to Masud Khan's perceptive and novel paper, "On Freud's Therapeutic Frame." Khan remarks that

> the classical psycho-analytic patient can be described as a person who has evolved enough maturity of psychic functioning and emotional development to be able to relate to another, sustain a minimum of trust and faith in the face of discouraging failure of communication, and who has, across his own development internalised the significant, experimental, interpersonal relationships with his environment, and can, when helped, give them symbolic expression. Those who did not fit in with these requirements Freud considered unsuitable, and they were the cases of madness or psychoses or those highly introverted, self-absorbed individuals who we call narcissistic character disorders. Of course, in the past four decades the situation has radically changed, and the refinement of Freud's therapeutic frame and understanding of how it functions has enabled us to take on cases in which much more demand is put on the analyst to *participate* in the patient's illness than was in the original, classical, analytic situation.

That too applies to the emergence of the new group psychotherapies, which also are dealing with another patient, a patient who could not possibly be reached in terms of Freud's therapeutic frame. That in itself does not dismiss Freud, as so many of the new therapists are tempted to do, but it simply adds another dimension to the whole field of psychotherapy.

Michel Foucault, who is perhaps the one scholar who has tried to define the crystallization of the psychiatric patient from the changing social frame across many centuries of cultural developments in

Europe, states very succinctly the whole issue of the new status of man in Western culture when he says in *Les Mots et Les Choses:*

> Une chose en tout cas est certaine: c'est que l'homme n'est pas le plus vieux problème ni le plus constant qui se soit posé au savoir humain. En prenant une chronologie relativement courte et un decoupage geographique restreint—la culture européenne depuis le XVIe siècle—on peut être sur que l'homme y est une invention recente. Ce n'est pas autour de lue et de ses secrets que, longtemps, obscurement, le savoir a rodé. En fait, parmi toutes les mutations qui ont affecté le savoir des choses et de leur ordre, le savoir des identités, des differences, des caractères, des equivalences, des mots,—bref au milieu de tous les episodes de cette profonde histoire du Même—un seul, celui qui a commencé il y a un siècle et demi et qui peut-être est en train de se clore, a laissé apparaître la figure de l'homme.

This discovery of man and self with a whole heritage on top of it enabled Freud to see that the patient was neither a bizarre social fetish or one to be endured as a familial nuisance. One of the great things Freud did for the psychoanalytic patient was that within the frame of the analytic situation, the analyst and the patient were unknown phenomena to each other, with no tradition of reliable shared symbols that could help them to negotiate with each other, and Freud had the integrity and the acumen to respect this paradox. I feel very strongly that in whatever therapy we are engaged in, be it the new group psychotherapies or the way-out individual therapies, we should not lose sight of this paradox, since it is essential to the engagement of patient and analyst. The desire in the new group therapies *to cut across*, so to speak, and to be on the line, honest and forthright, can only be accomplished with the same kind of integrity that Freud brought to the analytic situation.

Undoubtedly with the increasing rise in popularity of the various new group therapies many will come forward to claim their stake in the origin, history and development of these new therapies. Some of the more well known claimers are of course Perls and Moreno. At this point some reservations as to who really contributed significantly to the emergence of the new group psychotherapies should be made. Perhaps indeed it is not the time yet to single out specific pioneers in this new field. There is still a lot of maverick activity in the new group psychotherapies, and any credit in terms of the long-range history and origin of these therapies should be weighed carefully. As a matter of fact, Anthony[3] has pointed out in his reflections on twenty years of group psychotherapy at the diamond anniversary of the American Group Psychotherapy Association, maverick activity is generally experienced at the growing edges of a viable field, and what today may seem way-out may in the future be incorporated on a more solid basis into the main body of accepted theory and practice. Indeed the major problem is to explore how experimentation and innovation can take place without undue risk to the subjects who participate and how minimal standards of safety can be enforced. In tracing some of the historical roots of these new activities

---

[3]Anthony, E. J. "Reflections on Twenty-Five Years of Group Psychotherapy," *International Journal of Group Psychotherapy*, Vol. XIX, No. 3, July, 1969, pp. 277–301.

it is also interesting to note that the professional literature does not yet fully reflect the ferment in the field caused by this proliferation of marathons, encounters, sensitivity-training groups, use of nonverbal techniques and sensory stimulation in attempts to intensify, speed up, or increase the immediacy of the group impact.

Perhaps some of the historical roots of the new forms of group psychotherapy have to be traced to the nature of the American character, which we will discuss more in detail in the following chapter. Perhaps, too, some of the historical roots of the new group therapies are not all that historical and find their origin in the immediate past. I, for one, believe that most of the new group therapies are an outgrowth of the conventional group, which simply did not work any more for a considerable number of people (or perhaps they did not want it to work any more), while in turn conventional group therapy is an adjunct (and perhaps an outgrowth) of individual therapy. The designs of society and character have changed considerably over the past fifty years, and it is no wonder that each new decade brings us new openings, inventions and opportunities in the field of psychotherapy in general. To deny this historical trend would be silly. Another question is, does psychotherapy in general as a body of knowledge incorporate these new findings? Does it make place for tho new inventions and thoughts?

Admittedly, traditional psychotherapy (and that includes traditional group therapy) moves very slowly in absorbing the new trends in culture and society. We still are tempted to interpret our patients in terms of a body of knowledge and theory that was deveoped years ago. How many therapeutic schools really have worked with, for example, the rise in technology and its impact on the individual and society? The failure (and understandable failure, at that) of traditional classical therapy to come to terms with all the implications of a new patient in a rapidly changing society accounts for the appeal and rise of the new group psychotherapies. Those who for some reason or another could not (or often wanted not) get any satisfaction or (quick) results from the classically oriented therapies turned understandably to something else, something they think is at least better or more efficient and perhaps also less painful.

The historical roots of a lot of the group therapies is not so much a matter of the trends of the past but much more the failure of individual therapy to come to terms with the new trends in society, especially in terms of the new patients. I must admit that I really cannot be too hard on traditional therapy simply because its framework and reference do not correspond with what is required of men in a technological society. The complexities of today's patient and society are so manifold that one simply cannot compare them to the quiet surroundings of a patient analyzed in the 1920s or even 1930s. In all of this we also should not forget that the therapist, too, has faced significant changes in his approach to the patient and in his own standing in the therapeutic field. More and more we are beginning to realize that the problem of countertransference for the contemporary therapist, be it individual or group therapist, is highly relevant to his efficacy with his patient. Patient and therapist alike are much more a part of the world and are *subject* to the same kind of pressures, which often brings the patient to the therapist! Perhaps in the new group therapies there is room for the therapist to vent some of his own frustrations and feelings about *him* being there. This adds another dimension to individual and group therapy, but it seems that the new group therapies are better fit to deal with this type of thing than the therapies of the past.

AMERICAN CHARACTER AND GROUP THERAPY

One of the most remarkable studies on the American character in the last decades certainly was David Riesman's *The Lonely Crowd.* One of the major theses of the book is that the contemporary character of the American people and society is of an *other-directed* nature. The other-directed nature of the present American character and personality structure has interesting links to the current interest in group psychotherapy in this country.

One of the aspects of the other-directed individual is his sensitivity to the *clues,* or signals, if you will, from others and, in the main, from his peers. Much more than the inner-directed individual he is attuned to the opinions and attitudes of persons, around him. His desire to know what others think of him and his way of life, his problems, and so forth, is in a way a perfect setting for a group therapy session!

Americans, perhaps more than other people, are more *inclined* to reveal themselves. Self-revelation is by no means a disgrace or even embarrassing. On the contrary it took place (and often still does) in the revival meetings, in testimonial meetings of the Christian Science churches, in the early T-groups and in the various aspects of a middle-class society, where privacy has all but disappeared. Secrets are not to be kept. Questions about one's personal life have never embarrassed Americans.

This might account for the freedom and ease with which most participants in the various group experiences conduct themselves. The display of emotion and the encouragement to act them out, which is so much a part of the new group experiences, is very much a part of the American personality per se.

It is also true that traditional psychotherapy as much as traditional group psychotherapy does not necessarily provide *such* personalities with the emotional satisfaction they are looking for. That in turn might account for the fervent interest in this country in the post- and neo-Freudian therapies or for that matter the various way-out therapies that have sprung up at the periphery of traditional psychotherapy. It is perfectly obvious that the contemporary American environment does not exactly fit nineteenth century Viennese oriented psychotherapy. The cultural and sociological implications of American life, character and society are widely different from Freud's Vienna and his patients. Even more so the second and third generation of Freudian analysts have not been exactly eager to place the therapeutic establishment or for that matter classical psychoanalytic theory on the block or under close scrutiny.* That is in itself a sad commentary upon the intellectual state of Freudian analysis and analysts in this country, especially since Freudian therapy of itself is sound and often most revealing for patient and therapist. But *rigid* application of Freudian concepts or the distortion thereof (and many so-called Freudian therapists do distort the original theories and applications of Freud) does not meet the current needs of contemporary patients. Therapists too often are too *insecure* themselves about their skill and techniques (they shrink from any kind of experimentation), and so rather than try some experimentation or be inventive with their patients, they reject out of hand some of the new ventures in therapy. Often they base this on what they feel is ethical, especially when it comes to the taboos in psychotherapy such as physical touch, and the like, thereby forgetting that the field is rampant with stories about classical therapists who either slept with their patients or married them, who are either psychotic or psychopaths or, in short, still have severe personal problems themselves. That alone does not constitute a judgment, but it simply raises the question of why be so high-handed when there are severe personal shortcomings among many of our best therapists?

We have to face the fact that the American society has produced the *type* of patient who simply cannot be put in a traditional Freudian context. They cannot always face the rather *lonely* journey with their therapists, because they (in contrast to analytic patients of the past) have nothing to fall back upon,

*It is rather appalling that American classical analysts in general have so little insight into the changes brought upon society and in turn, into the patients they see.

perhaps even more so since so many therapists are deadly afraid to put themselves on the line or simply to be human with their patients.[1]

Perhaps it is true that the American character and personality lends itself more to the new group therapies. After all, classical, individual therapy required (and still requires) a sense of privacy and containment on both the part of the therapist and the patient. It seems little surprising that so little is actually known about, for example, Freud's patients.* They moved within the rather conservative confines of a nineteenth century society. Most were undoubtedly upper class, some of them, we know, were brilliant artists. But on the whole none of them breathed a word about their experience with Freud. And understandably so, they too were very much a part of the conservative upbringing, they too cherished the sense of privacy, which Freud supported. However, such is hardly the case with the new group therapies. Patients are only *too* eager to discuss their experiences in group or private therapy. They will discuss it with one another or with outsiders. The eagerness, sometimes, becomes acutely embarrassing when they exhibit their neurotic problems in front of everyone and want (or insist) to talk about them.

Where in traditional group therapy there was and is a continuity and commitment to each other's experiences, in the *one-shot* experiences, such as the

---

[1]See my remarks in my book, *Group Therapy Today: Styles, Methods and Techniques* (New York: Atherton Press, 1969), chap. 28, "A Note on the Participation of the Group Psychotherapist," in which I have developed some of the notions mentioned in this chapter.

*We, of course, have his own clinical reports (Freud's, that is), but we do have very little in the way of a report on the individual experiences of Freud's patients. What it was, for example, to be one of Freud's patients?

marathon or a weekend at Esalen, there is no such thing. One has to reveal oneself to total strangers, there is no preparation nor, for that matter, any continuation. This aspect of a *passing* experience is perhaps more significant than it seems. It fits somewhere the American style of personality and character which finds it difficult to commit oneself for any duration of time.

Impatience with the process of working through (in psychotherapy), so essential and vital to classical psychoanalysis, seems to have dominated many a prospective patient's concern in going through the one-shot experiences.

Of course Fritz Perls, et al.,[2] will deny that their therapy is instantaneous, and they reject the notion of "turning-on" therapy, but many patients, particularly those participating in the Gestalt experiences at Esalen, see the instancy and *immediacy* of the therapeutic group experience as one that holds the most attraction for them among the many aspects of the new group therapies. They are tired of being told that analysis is a process of "working through" and that such a process needs time and reflection.

Somehow it does not seem surprising that the new group therapies have made such an appeal to the American personality since they do advocate the *quick* or *radical* cure, or dealing in the here-and-now situation in a most decisive manner. That would appeal to Americans who somehow have always been impressed with "getting things done" and have been *pragmatic* in most aspects of their individual, political, economic and social life. It only seems surprising that the reaction to classical therapy came as late

---

[2]See especially Frederick Perls, et al., *Gestalt Therapy Verbatum* (Lafayette, Calif.: Real People Press, 1969).

as the middle sixties! True, we have had the post-Freudians with Erik Erikson, the neo-Freudians with Fromm, Horney and Sullivan, and the various applications to group therapy; sure, there were the Reichians and the Existentialists, but somehow they still embraced the Freudian frame of reference.

If one thing has changed it is the frame of reference. In the new group therapies the Freudian frame of reference has all but disappeared. One wonders sometimes if there is a frame of reference at all. One of the attractions of the new group therapies for many Americans is its undogmatic and almost "free for all" approach to the solution of human problems. And although some practitioners and supporters of the new group therapies would argue the point, I maintain that most of the new group therapies have no ground rules or even a sound theoretical frame of reference. That certainly does not diminish their importance or even effectiveness.

Perhaps Americans too are more inclined to resolve their problems in a group setting and *with* other people rather than on their own or in a structured face-to-face individual relationship. The idea of *groupism,* after all, is not entirely new and has been observed by quite a few social scientists. William Whyte's *The Organization Man,* which caused such a stir in the fifties, is still a pertinent commentary on the desire of Americans to function and *deal* in groups, resolve one's problems within a given group structure and even subject one's social, cultural, and even moral attitudes to the judgment of given groups and organizations. Let us face it, much of the 1960s hippie rebellion—the way-out clothes (now worn by the respectable people!), the drug scene, the loosening of our sexual morals (thank God), even the political revival movement of Eugene McCarthy in

1968—were all part of a stand against the organizational, *judgmental* structure of contemporary society. It is partly the result of the failure of the society itself to establish autonomy for its citizens and the young. Riesman warned about that a long time ago in one of the last chapters of his book *The Lonely Crowd.*

There is another aspect of the new group therapies that has ramifications in terms of the American character and personality. Through all the new group therapies runs an exhibitionistic trend. There is a lot of emotional *display,* which the group *allows* and even encourages to a point; there is a great deal of touch and physical encounter, a lot of play-acting, so to speak. Where emotional display in individual relationships might be frowned upon or even embarrassing to the individuals involved, and the same applies to the physical encounters (Americans do not touch!), or one might even be ashamed about it, the crucial point in the new group therapies is that they give such behavior or display *legitimacy* or simply approval.

The lack of personal intimacy (and the desire for it) is reflected in the new group therapies where finally the opportunity is provided to establish such intimate, albeit temporary, relationships. Even the subject of touch (and the interest in nonverbal techniques) is highlighted in the new groups. Where Americans on the whole reject physical touch in personal interrelationships, it seems interesting that one of the major attractions of the new therapies in general has been the introduction of nonverbal techniques.*

---

*A long story probably could be written on the fear (and anxiety-producing situations) of physical touch in social and individual relationships of Americans. It is a known fact that the Continental people are quite uninhibited (especially the

As a matter of fact, it seems interesting and significant that most of the new techniques in group therapy have more to do with "getting things done" (a typical American characteristic) and that the nonverbal techniques are more attuned to that particular attitude of Americans. Such nonverbal techniques include psychodrama, touch, sensitivity training, game therapy, and others, which all de-emphasize the rather long and often tedious process of talking things out.

One of the other aspects of the new group therapies is that new methods, techniques and innovations are being continuously introduced (since no rigid theoretical structure prevents it from happening), which indeed is also an indication of the nature and character of American society, where change is a *consistent* item of the cultural pattern. The group therapists by and large are free to judge what they would like to do with the group, what methods and techniques to use and apply. Such is also made easy since the new groups are generally transient and temporal. A marathon might last at the most three days, and no firm commitment really has to be made. There is no commitment comparable to the one that one has to make upon entering individual analysis or even traditional group analysis. The commitment to classical individual therapy and to traditional group therapy is strong and, moreover, is a condition for its efficacy and ultimate success.

Could it be that the firm discipline and long-term commitment required of the patient in individual classical therapy does not fit any more with many of our contemporary patients? If so, it could then

---

French) in terms of physical touch. Somewhere this is extremely important since it gives one the feeling of comfort, being at home and security, all being wrapped in one another.

explain many of the shortcuts to the road of mental recovery, which have emerged in the last few decades.

Could it also be that the rise and appeal of the new group therapies vis-à-vis the American character has a great deal to do with the desire to invent new ways (all the time) for handling problems? Traditional methods usually do not last long in the American society; even people do not last long in their jobs and, on the whole, permanency of any kind is a luxury. The sense of temporariness pervades many facets of American society and colors its character. Certainly there is no sense of permanency or continuity about the new groups. They come and go, and they do in effect fit well into the patterns of discontinuity in this society.

Thus, in effect, the sense of *encounter* is short and only temporary. The nature of encounter implies a sense of impermanency. This fits well with the general pattern of American social life, where social and interpersonal relationships are often of a temporary nature. Also in the new groups perhaps less emphasis is being placed on the therapeutic aims and what counts is more and more the here-and-now experience. In a society where one senses the lack of permanency, it seems rather obvious that *any* approach in group therapy that emphasizes the immediate experience rather than the long run or permanent results would have the appeal of experimentation for that society.

One of the aspects the new group therapies stress is the importance of *feeling*. The person is required to get in touch with his feelings and not to intellectualize his behavior. This too has implications in the context of the American character and personality. One of the main characteristics of alienated, detached and lonely people is their inability to get in touch with their feelings. So many Americans who put up a brave front of casualness and who appear to be easygoing very often are detached and *un*feeling individuals. As a matter of fact, I think that during the last decades that type of personality has become prevalent in our waiting rooms. These people do not give the appearance of being greatly disturbed; they often function quite well in whatever they are involved in, but they are detached from their inner feelings. They ask few questions and usually do not feel committed to anything or anyone. Curiously they do not even have anything to fall back upon. They have no pleasant memories, nothing to hold on to, hardly anything moves or affects them. One finds them among the young (making a firm exception for the McCarthy youngsters), but also among the young adults in their late twenties and thirties. For some of these people, if they have entered private therapy, it simply did not work. That probably has a lot to do with the kind of therapist they choose. Most contemporary therapists have a difficult time reaching that kind of patient. They themselves get negative feelings about such patients, and before they know it they are useless with these patients because of their own countertransference reactions. A lot of these patients have, so to say, been floating around not really understanding what was going on, still having somewhat a vague desire to do something about it. Social and political scientists, particularly when the history of the last two decades is going to be written, will discover that the decline in political and social commitment in this society, the rise of violence and often the senselessness of it, the absence of political, social and economic reform, the impending revolution of the universities, will have a lot to do with the absence of genuine goals, the absence of inspiring leadership (with the possible exception of John F. Kennedy, but that was far too short anyway) and that in turn this has affected the postwar generations. Add to this a war which has in the last decade poisoned the moral fiber of this society and one can understand that so many *aimless* people literally were picked up by the emerging group therapies. The least that these new groups did and are doing for these aimless people is to provide a forum, a place where they can and often are forced to vent their feelings about all this. Since Fromm proved a long time ago that the character structure of a given society is intertwined with the emerging personalities of that society, it seems clear that the present character structure has produced the type of people who on the whole are passive, indecisive, angry (although often covertly so), aimless and undirected. It should be emphasized again that such a character structure does not lend itself to the classically oriented therapies. After all, in classical therapy there is the prerequisite that the patient is verbal, articulate, even somewhat at ease with his neurosis; he often has considerable emotional and societal resources and he still is very much in touch with his own feelings. Contrary to what public opinion thinks, the patient in classical therapy *cannot* depend upon his therapist; on the contrary he himself has to work at the problem, and this often makes the therapeutic process a lonely one, since the therapist is not very supportive.

The contemporary personality, then, which presents itself to new group therapies looks for more direction, strength, assertion, the formulation of his problems, not only by the group therapist but also by the various group members. Especially in a time where everything seems to be ambiguous, the patient looks for directness and confrontation. Such a confrontation he can expect in the new group therapies and he certainly can expect to be shaken in his own passivity. What this ultimately does to his personality and to his functioning is of course debatable. Especially, the new group experiences are *passing* and temporary for the patients involved. But does that not fit into many aspects of contemporary American personality?

Another aspect that relates to contemporary American character structure is the relative permissiveness of the new group therapies. There undoubtedly is an encouragement on the part of the group therapists and group members to *permit*, so to speak, the patient to get in touch with his own feelings. In order to do this he often has to go through quite an acting-out period. In traditional therapy this acting-out period is highly structured and carefully watched by the therapist. But in the new group therapies where the process is accelerated there is little or no time for reflection; hence the acting-out is performed right then and there. There are various ways to do this in encouraging the patient to act out his anger, his love and all the needs he has not come to terms with. But in the short period of the group experience this patient might look upon the permission of the group as approval and hence will not feel much of a responsibility for what he is doing. After all he has the permission of the group (and therapist). Such a permission has its roots in the permissive society we live in. Social scientists for a long time have pointed out the permissive aspects of this society, especially in the educational area, but also in the whole sector of child-rearing.

Could it be, therefore, that the new group therapies somewhere connect with and are the product of a permissive society? It seems quite certain that now many more patients seek approval than many of the patients of the past. It also seems true that patients do not necessarily seek the *privacy* of individual treatment, whatever school of thought it might be, but rather put themselves in a situation where they are looked at, so to say, and where they are testing others in terms of their own behavior.

It also seems true that the new group therapies stress the *now* (after the Gestalt therapists) situation, but do they change the *now* situation fundamentally for the patient? Or are patients in these new groups just exposed to another adjustment therapy? I think these are valid questions, especially in terms of the American character structure and society. After all, patients do return to their environment after having attended the group sessions and they are expected to pick up where they left off. Are they now prepared to cope with the situation? Or are they prepared to change the situation they were in? Do they adjust or do they try to map out new ways and means to deal with the situation? Some of the Esalen people (and we will discuss this more in detail in Chapter 4) have been inclined to stay and work at the Esalen Institute or join Fritz Perls in his new venture (some kibbutz community) in Canada.

However, retreats have never solved the problems of individuals as to how to cope with their society and themselves. On the contrary, it is quite safe to say that all retreats always have ended up in miserable failure. Retreats on the whole are artificial in that they hardly reflect the society at large and thus do not prepare those who want to return to society.

In a certain sense, psychotherapy and group therapy have that same unreality about them. We should never forget that therapeutic sessions, be they individual or group, are artificially created. Even the relationships between therapists and patients and between patients and patients in group situations are to a large extent artificial. True enough, spontaneity and genuine feelings might emerge in these relationships, but do they last, and do they provide the patient with enough to go on after he leaves?

In returning to the relationship between American character and group therapy it seems safe to say that many elements in the American character structure are ideal for the appeal of the new group therapies; certainly, the pragmatic aspects of the new group therapies, their undogmatic, nontheoretical, approach to the solution of the problems of the individual in this society seem to coincide with the general characteristics of American society. Do they provide new solutions to the problems of the individual in this society is another question, which we will try to look at in discussing the various new therapies. Even so, the answers have to be tentative, since the new group therapies are just beginning to have some impact on parts of this society.

THE ENCOUNTER MARATHON

Of all the new approaches in group therapy the marathon has been the most significant one to date. The marathon has revolutionized the nature of group therapy almost overnight. It hardly can be labeled as a single technique in group therapy since it departs radically and decisively in form and content from the ordinary group-therapy group. In content it has broken with virtually every rule of traditional psychoanalysis in its approach to both patient and therapist. Indeed, one might argue, such rules probably would not apply anyway in a situation so far removed from the traditional psychoanalytic pattern. But then most of the therapists, at least (if not many patients also), were schooled or steeped into some form of conventional psychoanalysis. Even those who privately had left behind a lot of the rules and regulations of traditional psychotherapy and who quietly were experimenting with their patients, even those were still adhering to what was established and accepted in the field of psychotherapy.

For many therapists, therefore, the marathon meant a radical departure from the traditional approach in psychotherapy. And many are reluctant to deal with it or simply dismiss it as just another fad in psychotherapy. This is complicated with the fact that, although there is already a small literature[1] about the marathon, little is actually known about its background, history and methods.

Already many are claiming to be the first in initiating the marathon experience. As so often is the case there comes a point when the diffusion of ideas has in fact been instrumental in getting several people at the same time working on the same project or idea. In all fairness it should be said that probably Fred Stoller,[2] George Bach,[3] Bill Schutz[4] and Elizabeth

---

[1]For two very informative papers see George R. Bach, "The Marathon Group: Intensive Practice of Intimate Interactions," *Psychological Reports* (1966), 181, 995–1002. Also reprinted in Hendrik M. Ruitenbeek, *Group Therapy Today*, and Elizabeth Mintz, "Time-Extended Marathon Groups," *Psychotherapy* (May, 1967), Vol. 4, No. 2. For a more popular version of a marathon see Renata Adler, "The Thursday Group," *The New Yorker* (April 15, 1967), and a novel *The Lemon Eaters* by Jerry Sohl (New York: Dell, 1967). As yet unpublished a very good paper by Elizabeth Mintz, "The Marathon on Wings." And see also Eugene Alexander, "From Play-Therapy to the Encounter Marathon," *Psychotherapy*, (Summer, 1969), Vol. 6, No. 3.

[2]Fred H. Stoller, "Accelerated Interaction: A Time-Limited Approach Based on the Brief Intensive Group," *International Journal of Group Psychotherapy* (1968), Vol. 18, pp. 220–35.

[3]George R. Bach, "The Marathon Group: Intensive Practice of Intimate Interactions," *Psychological Reports* (1966), 181,

Mintz[5] in New York have been pioneers in introducing the marathon experience to the therapeutic field.

One of the first questions is, where did the marathon originate? What are the historical roots of the marathon, if any? Traditional therapy has focused mainly on verbal communication regardless if it was individual or group therapy. However we have come to discover that often words are inadequate to express the dynamic paradoxical intricacies of experience. Often words disguise, obscure, hide true feelings.

Eugene Alexander believes that some relationship exists between the marathon and play therapy. He writes:

> In play therapy with children this is not necessarily so (the hiding of feelings). In the first place, because of their limited experience with language, children often do not have the adult skill to use words either expressively or defensively. In the second place, children are more used to expressing themselves in action and direct involvement. In play therapy, children live in the immediate world of experience. They express themselves in the "here-and-now" as they really feel. The action milieu tends to bypass the reluctance and hesitancy that intercedes as feelings become mixed up with ideas, ideals, and expectations. Feelings emerge in their true tonal qualities. The play setting facilitates the ex-

---

pp. 995–1002. Also in Hendrik M. Ruitenbeek, *Group Therapy Today*.

[4]William C. Schultz, *Joy* (New York: Grove Press, 1967).

[5]Elizabeth Mintz, "Time-Extended Marathon Groups," *Psychotherapy* (May, 1967), Vol. 4, No. 2, also in Hendrik M. Ruitenbeek, *Group Therapy Today*.

ploration of experiences not accessible to awareness on a symbolic level; experiences that can only be felt and sensed, experiences that defy verbalization because of their contradictory paradoxical nature. The movement and contact in play therapy allow for the integration of bodily experience and bodily learning that is not available without activity. The manifestations of aggression and affection that are so hesitantly and tenuously expressed in everyday experience can be offered and shared in direct and immediate human contact. Fears can be faced, explored, experimented with, not in the abstract, but in their full force in direct human interaction. Words are spontaneous and part of the immediate experience rather than rationalized abstractions from it. Stereotype action and expression drops away and the child is often amazed at the new real self that begins to appear. The child becomes excited about himself, excited about his experience, excited about life. The excitement permeates his bodily actions as well as his spontaneous verbalizations. His whole organism experiences a sense of freedom and he expresses this freedom in his bodily movements and his involvement in play. This expression in itself becomes enhancing to further openness. Toys function as a catalyst to help focus the play toward significant experience. Play therapy becomes an intensive interacting living relationship between therapist and child. Together they live through the child's reality, share his feelings, venture the joys, the anguish, the search of relationship. Often as I struggled through the torturous groping of adults as they hunted to understand and express deeply felt impressions, I wished that

> somehow I could find a way to slash through all this verbal garbage and deal directly with experience. Oh, if only there were some sort of play therapy for adults. If only there were some techniques for doing and being, rather than talking about. Oh, yes, there was some doing and being in "talking therapy," but this was the exception rather than the rule and seemed to happen in spite of the words. An "intimate relationship" often took long to emerge. Oh, for the immediacy of the encounter that can happen in play therapy.[6]

Alexander touches on a very important aspect of the reasons for the marathon experience. Verbalization often is not enough or inadequate for the patient to express the many feelings he has. Also in private therapy the therapist often has quite a difficult time in getting through to the patient, in opening him up, in other words in getting him to come to terms with himself. George Bach points out that in group experience the group pressure often takes care of that:

> Clinical experience has shown the *group pressure*, rather than the therapist's individual interventions and interpretations given privately, is a major vehicle which can move people effectively and quickly from impression making and manipulative behavior toward honest, responsible, spontaneous leveling with one another.[7]

---

[6]Eugene D. Alexander, "From Play-Therapy to the Encounter Marathon," *Psychotherapy* (Summer, 1969), Vol. 6, No. 3. p. 188.

[7]See George R. Bach, "The Marathon Group: Intensive Practice of Intimate Interaction," *Psychological Reports*, Vol. 18, pp. 995–1002.

He also points out that customary groups (traditional group therapy, the hour and a half group) break up that group pressure. Patients, in other words, do get away from such pressure through the simple fact that the customary groups only meet for an hour and a half, or at the most two hours, and Bach emphasizes this point:

> Customary schedules of group therapy tend to break this experiential learning unit. One-, two, or even three-hour office meetings are not enough therapeutically, although staff time and fee economics make them universally accepted schedules. We have tried long hour groups and also weekend retreats and closely spaced groups (every other evening). With each of these schedules we noticed that there are always a few patients who "slip by" the experiences, always waiting and ready to level truthfully with their peers, but never quite coming out openly transparent in time for the group to get hold of them fully for feedback, confrontation, and pressure to change. These brief interrupted groups rarely generate the right amount and kind of *influence-pressure* to make a crucial impact on the resistance learner. The brief group is an ideal playground for time-wasting, psychiatric games such as diagnosing (labeling) safaris into phantasies, psychological archaeology, playing psychoanalysis with "transference" interpretation, collusive acceptance of people's irrational self-propaganda as to "who is the best therapist," "best patient," etc.[8]

This verdict on the traditional group is not altogether unjustified. As a matter of fact it makes a

---

[8]*Ibid.*

great deal of sense to therapists and patients, who have been exposed to customary group therapy for some time.

In comparing marathons and encounter groups with the traditional groups some questions are being raised. Is the ideology, as it were, of the marathon or encounter group fundamentally different from the traditional group? I believe it is. In the traditional group the orientation is primarily historical in that questions as "why" and "where from" are fundamental to the functioning and the concept of what therapy is about of the group. Thus the traditional group basically does not depart from the essential premises of classical psychotherapy. Some of the traditional groups might have been more open and flexible in seeking the answers to "why" and "where from" but they remain firmly within the context of traditional psychoanalysis. Such is not the case with the marathon groups. In the marathon group subjective truths are shared, irrational and ineffectual behavior appears incongruent, to be dropped in favor of new, more intimate, and competent behavioral patterns. The latter emerge and are practiced in the course of the marathon. Such orientation thus primarily is *ahistorical* and emphasizes the "what" and "how now" rather than the "why" and "where from."

Productivity is stressed in the marathon group session and such productivity (of every group member) is the therapist's mission, which he achieves by *whatever* means at his disposal. Again a departure of the traditional group: Where the group therapist is very much confined to the rules and regulations of conventional therapy, the marathon therapist *has* to depart and separate himself from traditional approaches to psychotherapy. As Bach has mentioned,

> One of the . . . missions of the therapist [marathon therapist that is] is to maximize group feedback and enhance the opportunity for genuine encountering of and exposure to group pressure. For these reasons the marathon is not unlike a "pressure cooker" in which phony steam boils away and genuine emotions (including negative ones) emerge. The group atmosphere is kept focused every moment on the objectives at hand: to produce *change in orientation* and new ways of dealing with old crucial problems (creativity).[9]

Such a mission of the therapist in the marathon does not resemble at all the traditional role of the therapist either in private or group sessions. A therapist faced with this kind of task has to be engaged with the members of the group, has to be there with his whole personality, his whole being and gestalt. He cannot afford to play the neutral therapist, but has to participate in the group activity. Hence the fact that very often marathon therapists consider themselves members of the group and do put their own personalities on the line and bring up personal experiences and anxieties about what might be going on in the marathon.

Fritz Perls illustrates this attitude in his participation in the Esalen groups that have adopted the marathon syndrome, where he remarks in addressing a seminar,

> So we don't need any more the year-long therapies. On the other hand, I am often very much over-estimated in what I am doing. I am not perfect, I am a son-of-a-bitch,

[9] *Ibid.*

> I am sometimes very nice, I am not onmipotent, I cannot produce any magic, so I have got very much my limitations and very often I find somebody coming forth who has no other aim than to show what a nincompoop I am. I know this anyhow, that in certain situations I am impotent, I am helpless, and I don't *have* to win.[10]

Such honesty is required from any therapist in conducting encounter or marathon experiences. Those who cannot bring themselves or are not prepared to take this stand should not be involved in marathon work. Of course such a forthright stand, brings great risks with it, but the nature of the marathon and the stakes involved require such a stand on the part of the therapist and the patient.

Another illustration of the personal involvement of marathon therapists and their impact on the dynamics of the marathon has been given by Robert Smith et al., where Smith attended a marathon conducted by a male and female therapist. Apparently the marathon got stuck in the conflict between the two therapists:

> Then, near the height of the gathering tension, a voice spoke from the far end of the room. The voice was that of a girl-woman, recently divorced, frightened of men and bitterly angry. She violently accused the male therapist of not being a man, of being too weak to lead this group, of failing in his responsibility toward himself and the group. I could feel a sudden cold stillness fall across the entire group, as if fear had suddenly

---

[10]Frederick S. Perls, *Gestalt Therapy Verbatim* (Lafayette, Calif.: Real People Press, 1969), p. 76.

crystallized itself into words. It was obvious, from his facial expression, that the therapist had been surprised at this outburst but was aware of the truth it contained: not as reflecting the personal needs of a person, but the personal needs of the group. He then began to speak slowly in a very soft voice to the female therapist, allowing the feeling to build slowly from within himself, attempting to maintain a rational grasp on what had transpired. I noted that while speaking, he was sitting slightly off center of the room resting on one arm, while she rose from her position in the corner, crossed the room and sat down beside him. She, in turn, began to express her feelings of disappointment in the marathon, and the direction in which she felt the group should move. He answered her with increasing anger recalling the instances in which he felt she had blocked his attempts to communicate with an individual, or instances in which she had shielded someone from further dialogue with him. He spoke of being most comfortable proceeding along a step-by-step approach to a problem area, while she seemed impatient and eager to take shortcuts to reach the same or similar goals. This last statement made her rise to her knees and swing around to face him directly. She expressed depression, a wall-between, and a sense of plodding frustration with his approach. There were things—important things—to be done with each person, she seemed to be saying, and they were destroying the moments.[11]

---

[11]Joan Fagan, Robert D. Smith, and Robert J. Timms, "Three Views of an Incident at a Marathon," *Voices* (Fall, 1968), p. 55.

The confrontation between the two therapists went on and the struggle between them symbolized for many marathon members the struggle between the primal father and the primal mother, and again I quote Smith:

> ". . . she lunged (the female therapist) forward catching him full around the waist, the force of her driving them both against the near wall. They both hit the floor and rolled over, coming to their feet almost simultaneously while still struggling and interlocked. The struggle reverberated in the mind like a slow-motion movie of someone falling from a tall building: the plight is horrifyingly real, but so is the terror of flailing struggle, frozen on the film of memory. It is difficult to know which is the less comforting end—defeat or self-knowledge. The only movement in the room was the heavy breathing and the physical sounds of two persons each trying to overcome the other. I managed to tear my eyes away to glance at the other group members: some were crying; others were screaming and clapping their hands at the same time; some angry because of the frustration in not being able to ignore it; some, so dulled and shocked by it, ceased to admit it and fixedly stared at the floor. But everyone with it. Everyone.
>
> The struggle lasted but a few minutes: although both were nearly equal in a physical sense, the male therapist finally achieved the advantage and forced the struggling female therapist over his knee and gave her a few solid whacks on her backside. The struggle was now finished: they stood up slowly, reached out to each other, embraced and kissed. I was finally able to tear my eyes

> away from them and through the tears and shock looked at the other members of the group. The faces of each member revealed they were identifying and dealing in archetypes that subtly evoke family figures, fathers and mothers, parent and child, lovers, the struggle between the sexes. Each person in the room saw the struggle as an explicit struggle between choice and fate. Who should win? Who must win? . . . from that moment on, throughout the remainder of the marathon, they sat together on the pillow holding hands, they went to each member as both mother and father, one comforting, the other holding, as needed . . . by their courage and struggle, they had defined the other's actions, became the other's purpose and mirror . . . There was a new vitality, a new spirit within the group. . . they had defined the framework of the basic conflict within each of us . . . in essence . . . this is the struggle: the primal mother and the primal father. Together in that small, dark room we were something more: the family of man.[12]

This experience shows that the leitmotiv of the marathon: "Show me NOW ... Do not tell me WHEN" is applied to everyone in the marathon. The here-and-now experience counts in the marathon, and *nothing else*. Telling the group about how one behaves outside the group and how "he" then and there reacted in bygone times and other places, back home or back at the office—this is only warm-up material. The thing to do is for each member to let himself feel his presence in the group and let the *currently active impact* of the others get to him!

By now some definite criteria have been estab-

[12]*Ibid.*, pp. 56–57.

lished as to the participants, the physical setting and the formal procedure of a given marathon. Marathon therapists in general accept outside referrals after an initial interview. There is general agreement that sufficient ego-strength should be part of the individual who participates in the marathon. Those whose reality-testing are seriously impaired should not be admitted to a marathon experience since they conceivably would crack easily under the group pressure. Some therapists, like the author of this book, conduct marathons only with their private patients, but the majority by now accepts outside referrals. A word of warning seems appropriate here. I think marathons on the whole should be restricted to those individuals who at least have had some previous therapeutic experience, be it group or individual therapy. For one thing it will make it far easier for them to work with gained insights and to make the marathon into a productive, personal experience. I know again that many therapists work with patients in marathons who have had no previous therapy experience, but I seriously question the ultimate effectiveness of such marathon experiences for the participants.

Usually the marathon starts at noon on Saturday and lasts pretty much about twelve to fourteen hours. The next day, Sunday, starts at about ten o'clock and lasts through the afternoon. The participants do not leave the premises except at night to go to their respective apartments for a night's sleep. Food, soft drinks and snacks are served. Fees usually range from $100 up to $150.

As far as participants of the marathon are concerned there are of course endless variations on a theme. But most marathons are mixed with some equal distribution of males and females. Somewhere

I feel that the marathon reflects our world experience, and that should be reflected in the marathon experience. One can put younger people with older people in a marathon, but I do not think those marathons work which have all males or all females.

The leader of the marathon should not only be well trained in conventional group techniques, but he should also have had a personal analysis. He should be in control of his own life experience, and his life style should be comfortable without too many personal problems. I have heard of rather disturbing experiences where untrained marathon leaders (with only the jargon at their hands) or outright psychotics have conducted marathons, brought in their own disturbing life picture and in a sense made the participants suffer for it. I firmly believe that merely participation in x-amount of workshops does not make an effective group leader. He should know about transference and countertransference and have a grasp of psychoanalytic knowledge. Moreover he should be able to diagnose quickly and effectively the patients of his marathon; his sense of analytic timing, which only can be reacquired after long and arduous analytic work, should be flawless.

The creativity of the marathon leader is extremely important for the successfulness and productiveness of the marathon. The author has conducted two types of marathons with his own patients. One has stressed more the verbalization of the problems of the participants; there is a great deal of life-history taking in such a marathon. The work in such a marathon is slow and often painful. Such a marathon is less spectacular to the participants than an encounter marathon. Not that such a marathon is devoid of emotion, but we arrive at insights through a more arduous process of "working through." Although physical affection and touch is expressed in such a marathon, there is less of an emphasis on physicality. In such a marathon, there is also less emphasis on the here-and-now situation of the participants. Their *total* life experience is under scrutiny.

The encounter marathon, which I have also conducted, confines itself strictly to the here-and-now situation. There is no life-history taking and the stress is on nonverbal techniques.

I would like to relate to the reader the experience of conducting such an encounter marathon where stress was placed on the employment of nonverbal techniques.

The marathon consisted of eleven participants, eight of them were female,* three were male. All had at least two years of individual therapy with me or another therapist. They all were part of the two traditional groups I conduct. I had told them that in this marathon we would employ the nonverbal encounter techniques and that no reference to their life history would be allowed. We simply would deal with our feelings in the here-and-now situation. I might add that such a marathon is in a way as structured as a verbal marathon!

We gathered on a Saturday at noon, and I asked them to sit down on the floor in a circle, close their eyes for five minutes, and move their hands to whatever direction they felt, that they were allowed to touch their neighbor, to push if they wanted to. Jane, one of my more advanced patients, broke the silence, since she had not been exposed to this kind of approach and, subsequently, infuriated one of the male participants, who had been to Esalen and knew the

*Since I only conduct marathons with my own private patients and since I do have a majority of women in analysis, the marathon reflected this.

game! He expressed his anger later on in the discussion of the exercise. "You ruined it, Jane," he said. Other reactions to the exercise were also interesting. Some of my patients thought that I had my eyes open!—although I had previously stated that I was as much a participant of the exercise. The two girls who sat on either side of me had serious feelings about touching me, which one of them did. Some of their fantasies in terms of their transference came through and it was extremely fruitful to have them out. Some people resented that others *invaded* their space (the exercise is called the feeling-space exercise) and felt that they were being invaded, put on, and so forth. Each one of the participants expressed his feelings about the experience, and it produced a great deal of material strictly in the here-and-now situation. John, who had been angry at Jane for interrupting the silence of the feeling-space exercise, was still angry. As a matter of fact he came angry to the marathon. Since I felt he was holding on to his anger, and was so to say "locked in," I asked the marathon to form a circle and asked John to put himself in the circle and try to leave it. Two things happened. Two other members of the marathon, Jane and Bill, got into a physical fight, in terms of kicking each other, when they were forming the circle. I will return to this later. John in the meantime had taken his place in the circle and tried to *smash* his way through the circle. Two of the girls tried to hold on to him, but finally they had to let him go.

The reactions to his exercise were manifold. Each member expressed their feelings about why he would not let John out of the circle or keep him in. Katy, who was the only lesbian girl in the marathon, and still had some quite unresolved problems about men, simply stated that she *would never* let him out of the circle and indeed she literally fought to keep him in! Then we returned to the fight between Jane and Bill. Relations between the two always had been strained in my group of which both were members. Jane felt that Bill was not really working on "his problems," that he had no notion or insight into what was going on. She on her part always got herself involved in relationships with men, which turned out to be very destructive for her. She almost seemed paralyzed in these relationships and was indeed at the mercy of these men, who on the whole were passive, subtly angry men.

I asked each of them to stand at oppostie sides of the room so that they were facing each other and then to proceed to each other and do anything that came to their mind. Bill remained where he was and Jane walked up to him, whereupon Bill broke the rule of nonverbal exercise and asked her, "Are you going to hit me again?" Jane did not answer and remained standing in front of Bill. Then an amazing thing happened. Bill took Jane by the hand and led her back to the group and practically put her back in her chair, thereby slightly touching her head as if to say "I am putting you in your place." The reaction of most members of the marathon was one of utter amazement. The question was raised "Why did you let yourself be put down?" Amazingly enough it had not even dawned on Jane that she had been put down. When it became clear to her that she had just *reenacted* her relations to men she became furious with herself.

The exercises, most of which are described by Schutz in his book *Joy,* proved to be very helpful for the members of the marathon in formulating and illustrating their problems. One of the girls, Margaret, had always had trouble in formulating verbally her problems and feelings. In this encounter marathon she cried freely and was very much in touch with herself and others. She participated in a group fantasy, and in her fantasy ran right into the rejecting men of her life, including her father. We did another circle exercise with Margaret, whereby she was outside the circle and had to try to enter the circle. She went to those members of the marathon she felt close to and simply took their hands and entered the circle. She related later how terrified she had been of a possible rejection and how this experience had illustrated to her her basic fear of being excluded, not being accepted, and so on. It should be stressed here, that the experience of Margaret was shared by all members of the marathon. Each of them had their own feelings of letting her in—or not.

I introduced in this encounter marathon a new exercise, heretofore not described in the literature, or as far as I know not being employed in encounter marathons. I called it the "transference exercise," and it obviously can only be employed effectively when one does a marathon with one's own patients.

I stood in the middle of the room and asked the members of the marathon to approach me, one by one, and do whatever they liked or wanted. The reactions were amazing, and in a sense the experience was exhilarating for me and the members of the marathon. Some members in discussing their feelings after the exercise felt that they finally had permission to hug me or touch me. Others were afraid and even terrified. One member of the group who competed with me in the marathon (he had attended Esalen on several occasions and felt that he knew!) and is an eager, young and successful producer and director, walked up to me and simply picked me up and in a playful way turned me around several times. He admitted that he wanted to express his power and authority over me. One of the girls, a lesbian, expressed her negative feelings toward me by passing me to sit down on a chair behind my back, where she quietly sat for a few moments. Another girl who always had very positive feelings toward me simply danced around with me. The members of the marathon then discussed again all their feelings vis-à-vis their own experience and their observations of others.

The importance of physical affection again was illustrated when we did the rock-and-roll exercise. The girl who was the subject of this exercise was and still is in a very destructive marriage. Her husband has been impotent for most of her marriage (twelve years) and she feels of course terribly deprived. She broke down in the marathon and we felt that she needed comfort and affection. We therefore stood in a circle and she went around and hugged and kissed everybody. It was a most moving and terribly important experience for her. It showed her, as we discussed it later, that she finally had to admit to her needs for physical affection and that she simply could not continue in a situation where she is deprived of the fulfillment of those needs.

The importance of the rock-and-roll exercise became evident later on when we literally rocked John after he had been on the hot seat and had broken down in his anger and furor. I had given him a pillow that he could beat. He finally was so exhausted that we decided to rock him. The reactions to this exercise with him were quite interesting since some of the members of the marathon felt quite negative toward him and now found themselves in the position to hold him and rock him (it should be stressed that *no* member has to participate if he does not feel like it). Some said that they simply could not see themselves letting him go (in other words letting him fall!), others experienced a great deal of emotion while doing the exercise. Schutz does mention in his book that this exercise is extremely emotional and that inevitably members of the group will start crying.

This experience with an encounter marathon showed me how effective nonverbal techniques can be in conjunction with individual and conventional group therapy. So many of the emotions of our patients are simply not being expressed in the conventional setting and the encounter marathon is a most valuable tool for the therapist to employ in bringing out these hidden emotions and feelings.

The encountering experience in the marathon actually is a four-phase process. Individual expressions are (a) reacted to, and (b) these reactions are shared in a "feedback"; (c) the feedback in turn generates counterreactions (d) from the original expressors as well as from the rest of the group. All members of the group are expected to participate. No one should wait to be "brought out." Everyone is expected to put himself voluntarily into the focus of the group's attention, to seek out the group and to turn attention to himself, preferably a number of times. This applies to everyone in the marathon—there are no *observers*, only *active* participants.

In the exchange and interaction between members of the marathon Bach feels that, "Candid leveling" is expected from everyone, which means participants explicitly share and do *not* hide or mask their here-and-now on-the-spot reactions to one another! Tact is "out" and brutal frankness is "in." Any phony, defensive or evasive behavior (such as playing psychiatric games or reciting old "lines") is fair game for the group's critique and verbal attack. "Ought's-manship" (advising others how to solve their problems) can deteriorate into a time-consuming, dulling routine which suppresses spontaneous encounter. Excessive advice-giving is, therefore, undesirable."[13]

In short, all the emphasis in the marathon is placed on the immediate experience. Come to terms with it right here and now, do not postpone, do not evade and above all do not hide. Tell me how you feel *now*, not tomorrow or yesterday. Trying to make people "feel better" is not the purpose of the marathon. Self-appointed, tactful diplomats, amateur "protectors" and "Red Cross nurses" distract and dilute the leveling experience in the marathon. Any kind of protective "cushioning" or cuddling spoils for the person in question the experience of standing up alone to the group, as he must to the world. Most important is that the members are expected to show themselves as they are in the world outside. As Bach emphasizes,

> The marathon group simulates the world of emotionally significant others; and the ways in which the member relates to this world reflect the core pattern of his being. The group members' reactions give cues as to the effect his behavior patterns have on the world. He has the option to try out new, improved ways of being.[14]

That does not mean that the group will not encourage a new found insight and affection is displayed there were it is necessary and to the point

---

[13]George R. Bach, "The Marathon Group."
[14]*Ibid.*

and as Bach observes "Reinforcement of new learning is the loving side of critical leveling."

But what about all this release of hostility, affection and dependency? How does the therapist manage all of this. After all most of the participants are relatively unknown to him (most marathon therapists admit patients after one or two initial interviews) and how does he know what reactions he is going to get and, even more so, how is he going to handle it? Elizabeth Mintz in her first paper on the marathons writes about the therapeutic management of these problems:

> The therapeutic management of openly expressed anger depends on so many variables that only a few possible techniques can be described. When the anger is exaggerated, or indicates a gross perceptual distortion, the group can be depended upon to stay with reality, offering alternate ways of perceiving the anger-evoking participant, or offering interpretations—usually valid—of unconscious reasons for the anger, having to do with family background ("Didn't you say your father was submissive too? Maybe that's why you're so burned up by his submissiveness") or with projection ("Well, frankly, you impress me as kind of effeminate, yourself. I think you're sore at him because you're sore at you"). The angry participant may then temporarily shift his anger to whoever makes the interpretation, and thereafter often spends some time in silence, perhaps assimilating the experience. Surprisingly often, the silence ends in friendly overtures to the participant who originally elicited the anger.[15]

---

[15]Elizabeth Mintz, "Time-Extended Marathon Groups," Hendrik M. Ruitenbeek ed., *Group Therapy Today,* Chapter 24.

Nonverbal techniques are highly popular in the marathon experience and, again, especially in dealing with anger such techniques might be very useful and as Elizabeth Mintz remarks,

> When the anger takes the form of intensely competitive feelings, along with the surface fear of being defeated which often masks an unconscious fear of winning, the competitive participant may be asked, "Who in this room would you most like to compete with? Or who are you most afraid of competing with?" The therapist may then suggest the nonverbal technique of arm-wrestling, which is quickly picked up by the group and utilized spontaneously as an auxiliary technique thereafter. This involves the competitors placing their two right arms together on the floor or on a table, elbow to elbow, and each attempting to force down the arm of the other. Nearly always, both competitors become intensely involved in it, and as yet the defeated competitor has never seemed to experience any resentment. Usually there is a mutual sense of exhilaration which spreads to the group. Often there are sudden, spontaneous insights as to the meaning of competition. ("I wanted to win, but God, I think I threw the match. My God, am I afraid of winning?") ("It scared me to beat him.") ("I felt as if I'd die if I couldn't win. Didn't know how set I'd be on winning.")[16]

That marathons put a heavy emotional strain upon the participants no therapist will deny, but it is interesting to note that the marathon group itself often takes care of the emotional needs of a given

[16] *Ibid.*

member. This is perhaps the most intense phase of a marathon group. With the natural sensitivity with which all group therapists are familiar, a group does not intrude upon a participant who is undergoing this deeply felt sense of strain, desolation and often loneliness, but accepts his feelings with warm silence. Almost invariably, one person, usually but not necessarily the therapist, offers physical comfort. When a mother figure or a father figure seems to be needed as the comforter, the therapist or cotherapist may put an arm around the shoulder of the grieving member or clasp a hand. Sometimes fellow participants are more appropriate comforters.

Elizabeth Mintz raises the question of the taboo of physical contact between patient and therapist, which is strongly adhered to in conventional therapy and she remarks,

> The question has been raised legitimately by colleagues as to whether this type of physical contact does not imply a direct libidinal satisfaction which may sidetrack the group from its therapeutic purpose, or lead to undesirable acting out. In the writer's opinion, physical contact under these circumstances is neither a direct sexual gratification nor an evasion, but rather a genuinely therapeutic corrective emotional experience. In our emotion-alienated society it is rather easy to find sexual contacts, even though they may be meaningless; but our tradition is quite consistently opposed to physical contact between adults which expresses affection, sympathy, support, or even simply human comradeship.[17]

[17]*Ibid.*

She relates that in a marathon session the use of physical contact often breaks the intellectual defenses, and she cites the example of a man who was describing the physical distance which his mother kept between her and the children. He was convinced that this distance had contributed significantly to his having difficulty in establishing physical experiences with girls that were emotionally meaningful. Dr. Mintz approached the man in the marathon and sat down close to him and then said to him "Touch me." There apparently was a moment of awkwardness and embarrassment, but once this was broken he was able to embrace the therapist and was very much relieved and joyful after the experience.

All marathons have their "cop-outs," their deserters, so to speak. Those are the people, well known to group therapists, who wait to be asked, who wait (and expect) attention, who often in their silent way are manipulative and scheming, who often are petulant and childish. They do pose a problem in marathons, but most members of a marathon know how to deal with them. I cite an example of Alexander, where nonverbal techniques were used in order to bring the member out. I quote:

> Attention begins to focus on Shirley. Nobody has really gotten to know her. Her range of feelings seems to be so narrow. Shirley is asked to give her impressions of people, they begin to sense Shirley's being and the *direction of her need* [author's italics]—Shirley, whom everybody likes and yet who does not get deeply involved with anyone. They want to see more feeling coming from Shirley, but she can't express feeling. And she says, "Help me." They ask her to cry and she can't cry. They feel helpless; they grope for a way to

lead her to the world of feeling. Someone suggests that she scream. She says she is willing to try to scream. Jim encourages her. She screams and screams and screams and then she begins to cry. A cry of anguish, a cry of release, a cry full of feeling. Nora holds and comforts her. Jim joins them and hugs Shirley. She cries for a long while with real relief. Then she looks at Jim and she says, "If you make me, I can cry a lot more." Jim responds, "Do you want to continue, or have you cried enough?" She says she has cried enough. Jim wonders, "Do you want to know how we feel towards you?" She says that she knows how they feel towards her. She feels their warmth. Jim persists, "Do you want to see how we feel towards you?" Hesitantly she says she does. Under Jim's guidance she goes into the center of the room. First one and then another comes and hugs her and holds her. Luci who tried to cry before and couldn't grasps Shirley tightly and they both cry together with a joy of open feeling. Shirley is feeling so deeply basking in the new world of aliveness. They join together, pick up Shirley and rock her gently, carefully, as she trusts her whole self to them. They rock her back and forth, back and forth, and it feels good. Then they gently place Shirley on the floor in a resting position. She lies quietly relaxing as she gets used to this new sense of being and awareness.[18]

Here the nonverbal technique almost has replaced the verbalization of psychotherapy and has produced feelings that are terribly important for the patient involved.

---

[18]Eugene D. Alexander, "From Play Therapy to Encounter Marathon."

But even in marathons where verbal techniques were still prevalent a totally different picture emerged as compared to the conventional group therapy sessions. The writer has conducted several marathons, all with his own patients,* and he has experienced that the verbal techniques if driven home (in other words, the patient does not get away with intellectualizations) to the very limit are still extremely useful. There is more time and it is up to the therapist to see to it that verbalizations take place and are concerned with the here-and-now situation rather than with rephrasing of the patient's history. Nonverbal techniques might be useful if nothing else helps. Those patients who are extremely resistant and who refuse to come out of themselves, who are unable to verbalize their feelings, those patients might find it helpful to explore some of the nonverbal techniques. However the pressure of the other marathon members often forces the silent or "deserter" member out of his corner. Also nonverbal techniques, useful as they might be, carry with them the notion of artificiality or play-acting, which should be avoided in a situation where we are striving for ultimate honesty.

Also contrary to the structure of conventional psychotherapy there are no established rules for conducting marathons. In other words therapists are relatively free in setting the stage for the marathon and are not bound by established techniques. Certainly for the sheer formal setting of the marathon a certain pattern has developed. Marathons usually are conducted over a weekend. Some, but not most of them, start on a Friday afternoon and last through

*The author has never accepted outside referrals for his marathons. Those therapists whose "specialty" is marathons obviously have to.

Sunday. The arrangements for sleeping are different for each marathon. Some therapists prefer their patients to be put up in nearby hotels, others simply send them home. There are of course marathons that do not have sleeping breaks, but serious questions can be raised here as to the ultimate efficacy of such marathons. Most marathons however start usually on a Saturday afternoon and last through the early Sunday morning; patients depart for their homes Saturday night and return Sunday morning, and the marathon continues until late Sunday afternoon. It is obvious that in such a setting where people have to be together for quite a long time the casualness of being together has to be stressed. People are urged to dress casually, to feel that they can move around in the room, no fixed seating arrangements, there are soft drinks and snacks available, and everybody should really feel that they are at home.

Since the marathon is unorthodox there is quite a bit of room for the employment of new techniques, and although most encounter groups still stress verbal techniques (with the exception of the Esalen groups, which we will discuss later) there seems to be a wide variety of techniques possible. Those techniques are more often not prescribed but are spontaneous and are often the result of the cooperation between the group members themselves. Elizabeth Mintz relates a moving experience from one of her marathons, which I would like to share with the reader, since it shows what resources a good marathon might have:

> Nick's history had made him especially interesting to me even before the marathon. He had been referred by his wife, Marilyn, a friend and younger colleague, who had married him only recently after a life of considerable personal tragedy. Nick's history . . .

had been tragic—a deprived childhood, a life of uphill hard work, and an unhappy marriage which he felt ethically justified in dissolving only when his youngest child entered college. Several years after his divorce, he married Marilyn—and for the first time, he was happy. They were endlessly congenial. Nick was successful, able to maintain two households. His children by his divorced wife loved and respected him. Then, with the irony which makes some of us wonder about Thanatos, came a major coronary.

When Nick recovered, Marilyn—herself a former marathon participant—called to ask me to include Nick in a marathon as soon as possible. His physician, said Marilyn, believed that he could stand the physical strain of a marathon, but that his way of life was so strenuous as to endanger his survival. Nick did not wish for long-term conventional treatment, and Marilyn hoped the marathon would reach him.

Appearing for the marathon, Nick turned out to be in his early fifties, burly, masculine, straightforward, likable. He smoked incessantly, admitting to three packs a day. He described an appalling work schedule. His physician, said Nick almost casually, had told him that his heavy smoking, plus his work schedule, was literally suicidal.

In the group, Nick had spoken of his situation frankly, but with reserve, although he showed warm interest in the other members. Nor did he seek the group's attention. Yet the group, with an unspoken agreement which is typical of marathons, now turned the spotlight full on Nick.

Without discussion, the members (none of them therapists) seemed to sense that Nick's self-destructiveness was not based on a lack of common sense, but on unconscious factors. They asked Nick to go round the room and say to each of us in turn, "I want to die because . . ."

Nick complied. As usual when someone performs this task, he found himself making statements of which he had been only half-aware. "I want to die because . . . I don't deserve to live. Because I've been a bad boy toward my parents. Because I'm tired. It isn't worth thc struggle. I want to die because . . . because no one would care!"

Now he was asked to go around again and give the reasons why he wished to live. This seemed more difficult. With pain, he said "I want to live because . . . I'm still strong. I have lots of life ahead. Because I love my wife and she loves me. I'm having fun, I'm a success, I'm happy. . . ."

Still lighting one cigarette after another, Nick told an anecdote. An old friend of his, taken with Marilyn's charm, had apparently tried shock treatment. "Every time you light a cigarette," the friend had said, "think of me in bed with Marilyn. Because if you go, pal, that's what I'll try for."

Knowing that suicides, direct or even indirect, often imply "I'll die and then they will be sorry," I picked up the implication of Nick's story. "I haven't a doubt that Marilyn loves you deeply, but it's true . . . she's attractive. If you died she could certainly remarry, if she wished."

Nick nodded, still unmoved. My co-therapist, however, was in touch with Nick on a deeper level. He saw that Nick was actually denying the possibility of death. Frank said, "I think we have to have a funeral for Nick."

With growing seriousness, the group created a scenario. A place was cleared for Nick on the couch, and he lay down as if within a coffin. The group played friends and mourners, saying their last farewells, but picking up the tone which I had struck.

Someone gave Nick a pack of cigarettes, instead of flowers. Someone also took one and lit it, saying, "He doesn't need it now." Someone said, "He was a good guy, but he's dead. Let's have a party."

Meanwhile Frank Rubenfeld (the co-therapist) stood silent. After everyone else had gone by he approached the "coffin." He moved slowly. With the curious intuition often seen in marathons, the group watched in total silence.

Frank stood by the "coffin," then dropped slowly to his knees. He reached and clasped Nick's arm. Then he bent his head and began to cry. It was not a pretense, nor was it the actor's ability to summon tears. Frank, a man who is not afraid of his feelings, was crying because he knew that Nick was throwing away his happy marriage and his newfound fun in life by risking premature death.

The moment seemed to last forever. Then Nick began to cry too. After a while he sat up.

"Enough already!" said Nick. "It's stupid to be dead." There was another silence. Then Nick, with wondering amazement, looked at us all and said *"It could happen!"*

The group stayed with Nick while he assimilated his experience. After that another man began mourning for his father, working through a grief which he had not been able to experience before. Nick sat on the couch, one arm around Frank's shoulders, one arm around the man in mourning for his father.

During the remainder of the marathon, Nick did not light another cigarette.[19]

It is also interesting to read in brief Dr. Rubenfeld's feelings about the incident with Nick in the marathon,

> I hit on the idea of the funeral as it became more and more evident that Nick had great difficulty in encountering his death wish and the reality of his dying within a relatively short time . . . . Where I surprised myself was in the depth of feeling engendered in me when I saw Nick lying as if dead . . . When I went up to him, I realized this is no shitting around, this man may die very soon. I cried for him because I liked him and it was sad to see him dead. And then, because it was real for me, it became real for him.

Elizabeth Mintz notes that no miraculous cures exist, and she adds that after three months Nick had not been able to give up smoking completely, but his cigarette consumption had diminished by two-thirds and that he was also working much less strenously.

The previous example shows the resourcefulness of a given marathon in dealing with a patient's problem. Note how there is no previous history taking, no questions about the "why" and "how," but there is a sense of immediacy about the whole thing. The patient is being put *in touch* with his own problem, he is made to experience the feelings of death, of separation, and right there and then he is made to experience the circumstances surrounding death. "Your

---

[19]Elizabeth Mintz, "The Marathon on Wings" (unpublished paper).

wife will take another" and "We will go on and have a party." The implication being that you might prefer to stay on for a while and enjoy your wife and the party! Note also how important it is that the therapist in such a situation is completely *with it* and shares the feelings of the patient. Dr. Mintz sensed it, but Dr. Rubenfeld acted on his feelings and participated with the patient in his misery about being dead. Such participation requires a therapist who is attuned to picking up the unconscious feelings of the patients in the group; he cannot afford to sit back and watch but has to, even more than the regular members of the group, participate in what the members of the group are going through. Indeed as Dr. Mintz remarks there are no miracles in this kind of an experience, but is there in long-term therapy?

But there are marathons and marathons, and the marathon described by Renata Adler[20] certainly does not sound like a very professional one. Even more so it seems that the destructiveness of the individual members is not being recognized by the therapist and that the members are simply there to vent a lot of hostility. If one compares the following episode from this marathon with the incident in Elizabeth Mintz's marathon, one senses a great deal of difference in tone, approach and sensitivity of those being present, and I quote:

> "A marathon was recently conducted in New York by a well-known psychologist from the West who had run more than twenty marathons in cities from coast to coast. The session had been convened . . . . by a hospital administrator from New Jersey, who brought

[20]Renata Adler, "The Thursday Group," *The New Yorker* (April 15, 1967).

along three members of his staff. The other participants were two young New York psychiatrists, one of whom had brought a troublesome patient, a middle-aged landscape painter, along; a television actress from California, who had been a patient of the therapist, and who brought her distraught dachshund; a receptionist from a brokerage firm, the group's only therapy novice, who arrived alone; a silent observer* invited by the therapist; and the administrator of a home for unwed mothers, who also arrived alone.

The session began at ten o'clock on a Saturday morning, in a single room of a suite on Central Park West. The members were introduced by first names to one another, and a list of rules was passed around and read. No one was to leave the room except to go to the bathroom; conversation was to be continued throughout the meals, which would be served in the room; no one was to go out of his way to protect any other member from verbal assault; and the identities of the participants were to be held in strictest confidence . . . . The first three hours of the session were spent in denunciations of the hospital administrator by his staff members. He was accused of megalomania, of eavesdropping on his assistants electronically in the name of "scientific research," of overworking his staff for the sake of expanding his clinic to become the largest of its kind in the country. After a long recital of grievances by one of the assistants (a man

*George Bach, whom one might call the father of the marathon, has remarked elsewhere that it should be a fundamental rule of a marathon that no observers are allowed, *only* participants (even the therapists do participate).

in his early thirties, dressed in white T-shirt, khaki pants, and sneakers), the administrator (also in his thirties, but wearing a dark cashmere suit) sighed and loosened his tie. He said, "What I'm hearing is this—proletarian envy and an infantile feeling of rejection." The assistant leaned back, and bit his fingernails.* Throughout this exchange, the therapist from the West, a chubby man in his early fifties, wearing a maroon sweater, a brown wool scarf, baggy pants, and loafers, had been sitting curled up on the floor, stroking the leg of one of the shy members of the staff under the trouser cuff.† "When are *you* going to say something, Harry?" he asked, in a heavy Middle European accent. "When are you going to *share* something with us?"

"Oh, he'll talk," the administrator said, "Harry never says anything until the twenty-third hour." The therapist resumed stroking Harry's leg. There was more talk. Lunch arrived, and the therapist homed in on the receptionist. "We know nothing about *you*, Elizabeth," he said. "Come, *share* something with us." The receptionist, wearing black net stockings, loafers, and a skirt belted at the hips and looking rather ill at ease, gave a brief outline of her early life and education, and, after a moment's hesitation, a description of a young man with whom she was going out at present. "You bore me," said one of the New York psychiatrists. The reception-

*Question: Why did not the therapist follow this through? Why leave the assistant with his obvious resentment? Why not explore this more?

†Question: Physical contact is fine in marathons, but why did no one raise the question as to why the therapist stroked the leg of the man?

ist looked nervously about the room. "I don't know what you want me to say," she said. "I'm so afraid something *awful* is going to happen." "Well, Lizzie," the therapist said, "you must share *more* with us than that. I warn you, if you allow nothing to *happen*, after the session you are going to feel depressed. Very depressed."* "Gosh," the receptionist said, smiling† awkwardly and casting an alarmed glance about the room. *No one smiled* back.** "What are you *smiling* for, Lizzie?" the therapist asked. "Are you really very happy at this moment?" "And you might cut out that 'Gosh' number, too," said the actress, suddenly springing to life. "You're a big girl now.†† What did you come here for? Aren't you interested in becoming a real person?" The receptionist choked and said nothing. One of the New York psychiatrists lunged across the room and took off one of her loafers. "Maybe that will loosen you up," he said, looking at the therapist. The girl sat frozen, with one loafer on, and abruptly re-

---

*What the therapist is doing here is not only absolute nonsense but it also shows a total lack of insight and feeling for the patient. The receptionist provided him with a very significant statement, "I'm so afraid something *awful* is going to happen." Why did he not follow this cry for help? Why not pursue with her what she felt about what might happen? Instead he punished her and told her she was going to be very depressed if she was going to keep this up. Well good for her! She was left with *nothing*.

†Smiling is close to being tearful and the therapist failed to pursue this point.

**That no one smiled back should have an indication to the therapist that the marathon was not a giving one. Although the receptionist was obviously going to have a rough time there was no ally in sight.

††Who said she was a big girl? That was the actress' observation or statement. Many people are still children when they are adult.

crossed her legs. "Perhaps you ought to take your skirt off, too," the therapist said, rolling his eyes. "Perhaps then you could share with us." "I don't know what you want me to say," she said, now close to tears.†

At one moment the therapist turns to the actress and said the following, "Diana is a very *special* patient," the therapist said, turning to the actress. "And I want to *share* this with you. I once made advances to her, and she turned me away. When she left our group in the West, she was given a trophy for being the most giving and sharing member of the group. Tell them about yourself, Diana. Diana is a very serious artist."*

Diana began to weep—[Why? she was just complimented as one of the star members of group therapy and on top of that she was a very good artist. What more could she want? Apparently it was not good enough. Or perhaps she sensed the phoniness of the therapist?]—and remained in tears for the rest of the session. It turned out that she was a kind of therapy nomad, traveling from group††

---

†No one picked her up on this statement, which she had said before. "What do you want me to say?" But they actually wanted her to take off her skirt and she did *not react* to that. Why? The therapist again obviously did not pick this up.

*What rubbish! Why did not the group explore the feelings of the therapist towards Diana. After all he approached her and made it a part of the introduction and ended up putting her down in a very subtle way.

††The sadness of it all does not come through. There she was traveling from group to group all over the country and no one was able to help her. Certainly a sad commentary upon the therapists who took her on and who no doubt are critical of orthodox psychotherapy. But at least in orthodox psychotherapy the therapist does not desert the patient but stays with her. Also what difference is there in the end between those who go from one individual therapist to another and those who go from group to group?

> to group, and that she had not yet lit in a group in New York. (One of the New York psychiatrists immediately handed her his card.) ‡[21]

Several comments should be made after reading these excerpts of Renata Adler's report of this marathon. First I do not think that any therapist should intrude on his patients with his own neuroses or, as they say nowadays, his own hangups. Patients do not pay to listen to the troubles of their therapists, at least we have not yet reached that stage! I find it highly disturbing when therapists attend marathons of other therapists (colleagues, that is) with their own troubled patients, as happened in this case. Moreover the degree of emotional involvement of these therapists with their patients is obvious, and I think of the wise words of my colleague Prof. Ernest van den Haag who once remarked to me that the making of a good therapist is determined by how he handles his countertransference. I must say that in this instance the therapist was unable to handle the countertransference problems involved and no marathon is going to solve that for him. Moreover any therapist with countertransference problems who does not proceed to solve these is doing a great injustice to his patient. His patient is entitled to his care not his problems. In the marathon as described and reported by Renata Adler it lacked the care and concern that existed in the marathon of Mintz. Also one wonders what criteria did the therapist of Adler's marathon set for himself in admitting patients to the marathon. George Bach

‡Did anyone comment on this callous act? Why give her his card? Why not participate and try to help there and then in the here-and-now situation.

[21]*Ibid.*, p. 78.

elsewhere has stated specific qualifications for a patient in order to be admitted to a marathon. Does a marathon need a therapy nomad as happened to be the case in this marathon? No, group therapy nomads suffer probably from the same kind of disturbance as those who will travel from one therapist to another. It is a problem in itself that they make changes, and unless they for once stick with it and try to work it out they will forever travel and go nowhere.

Obviously in the marathon of Adler the receptionist was an easy target, she did not measure up to the rather sophisticated bunch of people gathered at that apartment on Central Park West. What is maddening, though, is that the therapist did not single this out and did not try to help her. That is not protection, although I believe that even protection against severe verbal attacks might be called for, but merely a question of fairness and insight. Compare also the physical closeness of Nick with Dr. Rubenfeld after they went through the "funeral ordeal" and the rather meaningless gesture of the therapist in the Adler marathon in stroking the leg of Harry for no obvious reason.

All of this raises the question of how effective marathons are. The writer feels, having conducted marathons only with his own private patients, that they do provide patients with extremely valuable insights, insights which they would only have been able to attain in private therapy after a long time. However insights *alone* do not make the patient tick, and he still has to work them through in his own life style. What happens to marathons where the therapists recruit the patients from outside referrals (and those are the most usual ones)? I have little evidence to date to make substantial statements. Elizabeth Mintz maintains that the follow-up looks good and that on the whole patients retain quite a bit of what they have gained in the marathons, and she writes,

> . . . participants almost unanimously speak of marathons, immediately afterward and a year afterward, as a worthwhile and moving experience. The words "I felt reborn" are often uttered. At the very minimum this type of group has the stimulating and enriching impact of any intense emotional experience shared with other people. There is only anecdotal evidence as to the value of marathons. ("I went home and felt closer to my wife than in years." "I left feeling so strong; I still feel so strong." "I went home and discovered my kids don't really hate me. Ever since the marathon they like me. They come up to my desk and ask me questions.") and she adds "In the absence of objective measurements, notoriously difficult here as in other forms of psychotherapy, one may legitimately question the enduring benefit of an experience lasting only two days.[22]

There is something what I call a "marathon high." Patients are lifted by the very intense, close, emotional experience and they often go beyond themselves in acquiring certain insights and enjoy it too! But there is a certain euphoria which slowly wears off and then the patient has to be ready to face himself all over again. And in most instances he is on his own and cannot rely anymore for further probing upon the group. Some of course attend as many as three or four marathons and consequently do get a better picture of what is going on in themselves. Then again one has to realize that marathons and

[22]Elizabeth Mintz, "Time-Extended Marathon Groups."

encounter groups probably reach at this point those patients who would never enter individual or conventional group therapy. And probably they make up the bulk of today's encounter patients, and it is precisely for those patients that marathons came about and that they, although in a limited way, work. There is no doubt that little probing *in-depth* is being done in the marathons, and perhaps this kind of patient might be better off without it. Why upset the apple cart? Probing requires "working-through" and that in turn demands a long-term (or at least a reasonable) commitment on the part of the therapist.

It is also true that in an alienated and estranged society like ours the alienated look for quick answers and are impatient (and, do not forget, most of them cannot afford to wait) with themselves and society. The marathon provides them with a small society all for themselves where they can express themselves, where they can experiment, where they can come to terms with age-old taboos in their own and other people's lives. They do recognize the pressures of a marathon, they are even afraid of it, but they are also accustomed to it. The pressures are there, in society, all around, and the difference with the marathon is that they are able to confront it once and for all. Then they can reject it and curse it. They can live and act out their long-time fantasies, to talk about it and not be condemned for it.

Such are the advantages of the marathon, and they have given contemporary therapy another face and also a taste of what is to come. We are moving away from the strictly individual-oriented therapeutic sessions, how valuable they still are and will continue to be, to a more open and group-oriented and experimental form of therapy where some of the old adages of the past will not work anymore. It puts a totally different light on the contemporary patient and, let us not forget, also on the contemporary therapist. Most therapists have not even arrived at the point where they will consider these changes and ponder them. The therapeutic community better take note, the time is getting late.

THE ESALEN EXPERIENCE: A TRIUMPH FOR GESTALT THERAPY?

In the increasing flood of new group therapies, and mainly among the marathons and encounter groups, the Gestalt therapeutic-oriented approach to group therapy, as practiced by Frederick Perls and others, has been the most astute and perhaps successful of them all. In a sense it seems amazing how quick the Gestalt approach of Perls has caught on. Even a decade or so ago Gestalt therapy and Perls, for that matter, were virtually unknown. It is true that Gestalt therapy is especially effective in groups, and perhaps the wide popularity Gestalt therapy enjoys at this moment is due to the fact that the appeal of group therapy per se is by now almost overwhelming.

Gestalt therapy is closely related to the approach of existential analysis. Both forms of therapy stress the here-and-now situation and both encourage the element of *confrontation* is the analytic situation. If there is anything different between the forms of therapy then it is perhaps that the Gestalt therapists stress more the element of *feeling* in the analytic process and also the *contemporary* aspects of the process of psychotherapy. The Gestalt therapists de-emphasize or debunk the past and pay little attention to the future. Also they do want to establish what Perls has called the *continuum of awareness* in order that the most important unfinished situation will always emerge and can be dealt with.

Perls describes this continuum of awareness in the following words:

> This continuum of awareness seem to be very simple, just to be aware from second to second what's going on. Unless we are asleep, we are always aware of something. However, as soon as this awareness becomes unpleasant, most people will interrupt it. Then suddenly they start intellectualizing, bullshitting, the flight into the past, the flight into expectations, good intentions, or schizophrenically using free associations, jumping like a grasshopper from experience to experience, and none of these experiences are ever *experienced,* but just a kind of a flash, which leaves all the available material unassimilated and unused.[1]

There is a stress in Gestalt therapy on the *whole,* and the Gestalt therapist tries to take care of the

---

[1]Frederick S. Perls, *Gestalt Therapy Verbatum,* p. 51.

holes or filling in the holes, as Perls likes to call it. In their book *Gestalt Therapy*, Perls, et al., writes specifically about the therapeutic situation in the light of the Gestalt theories.

> The greatest value in the Gestalt approach perhaps lies in the insight that the *whole determines the parts*, which contrasts with the previous assumption that the whole is merely the total sum of its elements. The therapeutic situation, for instance, is more than just a statistical event of a doctor plus a patient. It is a *meeting* of doctor and patient. If the doctor is rigid and insensitive to the specific requirements of the everchanging therapeutic situation, he will not be a good therapist. He might be a bully or a businessman or a dogmatist; but he is not a therapist if he refuses to be a part of the on-going processes of the psychiatric situation. Likewise, the patient's behavior is dictated by many variables of the interview, and only the 100% rigid or the insane (oblivious of the context in which they operate) will behave in the consulting room as they do outside.[2]

The Gestalt therapist mainly moves in the NOW and has little use for the unconscious. As a matter of fact Perls states it unequivocally:

> . . . the simplicity of the Gestalt approach is that we pay attention to the obvious, to the utmost surface. We don't delve into a region which we don't know anything about, into the so-called "unconscious." I don't believe in repressions. The whole theory of repressions is

---

[2]Frederick S. Perls, et al., *Gestalt Therapy*, pp. xi–xii.

> a fallacy. We can't repress a need. We have only repressed certain expressions of these needs.[8]

This is a radical departure from conventional psychotherapy, and it adds a different dimension to the Gestalt approach. Gestalt therapists are not only concerned what the patient expresses, but also look closely to his body movement and listen to the sound of his voice. Again Perls, says, "A good therapist doesn't listen to the content of the bullshit the patient produces, but to the sound, to the music, to the hesitations."

Just a word or two about the three most mentioned people in this chapter: Frederick Perls, Bill Schutz and Bernard Gunther. Perls received his M.D. in 1921 from the Frederich Wilhelm University in Berlin. He was subsequently trained at the Psychoanalytic Institute at Berlin, Frankfurt and Vienna. In an interview with Dr. James Simkin, Perls relates his first encounter with Gestalt Psychology.

> I met Laura [his wife] in Frankfurt-am-Main in 1926. I was assistant at the Kurt Goldstein Institute for brain-injured soldiers . . . This was an amazing circle, Frankfurt-am-Main, at the time. It was really. The Existentialists and the Gestaltists! But at that time I didn't have much contact with the existentialists like Buber, Tillich, and ah, who else was there? Scheller, the philosopher. I heard his lectures, but the thing that fascinated me was the Gestalt approach. For the first time, the breaking away from the piecemeal consideration and getting perspective. And

[8]Frederick S. Perls, *Gestalt Therapy Verbatum*, p. 53.

> Kurt Goldstein was the first one who revolutionized neurology, from the point of view of Gestalt psychology . . . I started working with the psychoanalysts 'round about 1925. At first analysis with Karen Horney. I went to Frankfurt and worked with Clara Harpel and then Clara Harpel maintained that I was ready, and I went, was in '27, I went to Vienna for supervision work. We worked with Helena Deutsch, Hitschmann. . . . I was still very much involved with psychoanalysis. I worked first with Harnick, yeah, and then, ah, I worked with him about a year and a half and I couldn't get on with him. He never spoke or I felt what he did say was definitely sterile, so I went to Karen Horney and discussed the situation with her and she told me the only guy she thinks could be my match would be Wilhelm Reich. So I went into therapy with Wilhelm Reich which was about the ninth month up till the time that Hitler came. And with Wilhelm Reich I felt that I got something at least; I got into seminars and got my first active patients. And I also remember that in a seminar with Karen Horney she was very satisfied and pleased with the way I'd taken some case from the characterological and personality issue rather than from the complex and memory view. . . . [4]

During World War II Perls spent his time in South Africa, where he worked at the South Africa Institute of Psychoanalysis. He also met here Princess Marie Bonaparte, who had left France and as a member of the Greek royal family came to South

[4]Interview with Dr. Perls by Dr. James Simkin—AAP Tape Library Volume No. 31.

Africa with them in exile. Apparently she was highly critical of Perls, since she felt that he was disavowing orthodox phychoanalytic theory. After reading Perls's book *Ego, Hunger, and Aggression* she remarked to Perls, ". . . if you do not believe in the libido theory anymore, you better hand in your resignation."[5][!]

Eventually Perls and his family moved to the United States, where Perls worked in private practice in New York, Miami, Los Angeles, Cleveland and San Francisco, and in 1964 he started conducting training workshops and seminars at the Esalen Institute until 1969. He finally moved to Vancouver, B. C., where he was working at the formation of a therapeutic commune. His death just a month or so ago terminated a most fascinating participation in the complex world of psychoanalysis.

It should be stressed here that the career of Perls illustrates the precedence of Gestalt therapy over the work now being done at the Esalen Institute. Gestalt therapy has its roots in the early work of Kurt Goldstein, but also draws significantly from the work of the existentialists. Perls confirms that himself in the previous interview. Both Gestalt therapy and existential therapy stress the here-and-now situation. They emphasize the *Eigenwelt* (the relation to one's self) rather than the past or future. I think that the significance of the roots of Gestalt therapy serves to illustrate that a lot of what is being said or done in the realm of the new group therapies already existed in the minds and works of many existential therapists. Thus the Gestalt therapy derives a philosophical structure from the existential orientation, and I should stress here that both Gestalt and existential

---

[5]*Ibid.*

therapies are far more structured than many people now realize. In reading some of the case material of the Gestalt therapists[6] I felt again that their approach is basically *directive* and structured.

In terms of the roots of Gestalt therapy it is interesting to note that Richard Wallen feels that a great deal of the roots of Gestalt therapy can be found in Otto Rank,

> . . . it is only fair to say that this approach (Gestalt) to the therapy process represents one of the great streams of psychotherapeutic thought that stems from Otto Rank, who influenced Carl Rogers's client-centered therapy in a somewhat different way. Rogers's followers were interested in the present situation, too. They also focused on what the client was doing, but they never did get to the problem of the real *awareness* of what was happening to the patient *at this instant* . . .[7]

Bill Schutz and Bernard Gunther arrived on the scene much later than Perls. Schutz is primarily known through his book *Joy*, in which he describes and analyzes some of the techniques used at Esalen. His book certainly is an outgrowth of Gestalt therapy. Schutz at one time taught at Harvard and at the University of California. He has also advised on group behavioral problems and conducted small training groups for many public and private institutions, including the RAND Corporation. Bernard Gunther

---

[6]See Joen Fagan and Irma Lee Shepherd, *Gestalt Therapy Now* (Palo Alto, Calif.: Science and Behavior Books, 1970).

[7]Richard Wallen, "Gestalt Therapy and Gestalt Psychology," Joen Fagan and Irma Lee Shepherd, *Gestalt Therapy Now*, p. 12.

was once a body builder and ran a gym in Santa Monica. He is the author of *Sense Relaxation*, which essentially presents the reader with the exercises of the Esalen Institute, with which Gunther is associated. Vivian Gornick in her series on the new therapies for the *Village Voice* interviewed Gunther in a rather critical manner,

> I asked him to tell me about himself, where he was from, how he had come to this work, what he had done before. . . . "I'm from Los Angeles," he said softly, "born and raised." . . . "I used to be a body builder. A weight lifter. In Santa Monica. I ran a gym there. I was once 40 pounds heavier than I am now," he smiled. . . . "Really!," I said. (My God, I thought, am I hearing right? Has he just said what I think he's said?) "But somehow," he went on, "I never really felt good, never felt satisfied or alive inside myself. I tried acid, and for a while I really grooved on that . . . . And then one day I read Fritz Perls's book, and that was it. I started to do some real thinking. I began to see all the things inside myself I would understand if I was *aware*, *aware* of my body; I went to see him, I worked with him, and here I am.[8]

The great opportunity however for the Gestalt therapists came when the Esalen Institute emerged. Esalen is the name of an Indian tribe that once dwelt along the California coast. The Esalen Institute is a nonprofit, idealistic and controversial establishment dedicated to "devising ways to extend the hu-

[8]Vivian Gornick, "The New Therapies: A Brief Encounter," *Village Voice* (January 22, 1970), p. 10.

man potential." Its methods are varied, but are likely to include group therapy, psychodrama, massage and Oriental philosophy. It offers to the public weekend seminars (attracting an average of seventy-five participants at sixty dollars, including room and board) and five-day workshops ($155 to $175, with an average attendance of twenty-five). In addition there are about twenty-two resident fellows enrolled in a nine-month course ($3,000) in Esalen techniques.

According to Dr. John Downing, a psychiatrist and director of the San Mateo County Mental Health Services, the psychotherapy of *therapy*, period, is not Esalen's primary function, and he explains, "It is the concern of psychiatry to adjust people to the social environment. Esalen, rather, is concerned with those who are too well-adjusted, too tight and controlled. It attempts to release them for growth and greater integration."

Three people stand out in the Esalen experience. First of all there is Fritz Perls, popularly called the prophet of the NOW, then there is William Schutz, whose book *Joy*, has become one of the standard works for Esalen and for the whole encounter experience in this country. Finally there is Bernard Gunther, whose book *Sense Relaxation*,[9] completes a threesome.

Of the three there is no doubt that Perls is the most well known and probably the most controversial one. Rasa Gustaitis has given a vivid picture of Perls at work in her book *Turning On*. She is obviously impressed with his work but she allows for some criticisms,

---

[9]New York: Collier Books, 1968.

> Later, with other people, I will see Perls yawn openly, even fall asleep when bored, but . . . his responses are always genuine . . . The same is true of his behavior outside the seminar room. It is often rude, arrogant, inconsiderate—sometimes even outrageous. But he is always himself. Often he refuses to acknowledge any other encounter than one that is completely natural and direct. This means that some people, including myself, at times freeze into rigid nervous hulks in his presence. But I will remember these dreadful moments later as educational . . . I search out Perls in the dining room to ask him some theoretical questions. He seems willing to converse until I begin, "Are dream figures always *alienated* parts of the self? It seems to me that . . . " Perls lifts his hand in a gesture that stops me in mid-sentence. There is a pause. "Fine spaghetti today," he says pleasantly. But I turn mute. He has shattered my self-confidence.[10]

It was probably the directness and the no-nonsense approach of Perls that shattered Miss Gustaitis. This is one of the characteristics of the encounter approach (and, indirectly, the Gestalt approach), to cut through the garbage, as they prefer to call it.

Listen to him (Perls) putting a married couple on the spot about their feelings,

> He: I don't think I care to, Fritz. Unless, of course, you want to, Sally? You want to? (He's peremptory).

[10]*Turning On*, p. 31.

She: Hm. I don't want that question. It's okay.
Perls: He sounds like a blackmailer. Is he a blackmailer?
She: I don't understand.
Perls: You know what a blackmailer is. A Jewish mother is a blackmailer: "I don't care if you don't come home, do whatever you like."
She: I don't understand. I feel I'm in the middle of something of my own doing. I love my husband very much.
Perls: Say this to him.
She (leaning toward him): Julis, I love you very much.
He (without looking at her or moving): I love you very much.
Perls: In that position? Look at that posture! What a love posture! Could you by any chance be afraid of your feelings?
He: I don't think so.
Perls: What do you dislike about me?
He: I think you're obnoxious.
Perls: Now we're getting somewhere.
He: You're a dirty sloppy old man.
Perls: Ye-es? (He's enjoying this.)
He: At times I see a spark of some considerable ability in you. But I've watched you behave and you just don't measure up. I don't think you project yourself. You're too wrapped up in Fritz Perls.
Perls: Tell me what I should be like. (He is definitely enjoying this.)
He: You showed each couple how to project what they feel toward each other. Can you do that for yourself?
Perls: I'm pretty mean to hold myself back?

He: I don't know that you're mean. I just expected more of you.
Perls: Aha! Now we're getting somewhere. I don't live up to your expectations. I should be different than I am. Could this by any chance be the case with your wife, too?
He: No, my wife is a very-go-lucky kind of person. (The woman beside him looks timid, haggard and tense.)
Perls: Say this to her.
(He does, without looking up.)
Perls: Is he right?
She (after a pause): I'm afraid to get angry. (Pause) But boy, sometimes I do. (There is fury in her voice.)
Perls: Repeat that.
She: When I get mad—boy, sometimes I get mad and I feel good. (Her voice is full of rage.)[11]

Perls's objective in this case has been reached. Show them where they are at. Let them get in touch with their feelings.

William Schutz, even more than Perls, stresses the nonverbal techniques in dealing with contemporary patients and feels that "words are special culprits in the effort to avoid personal confrontation. At times, when a real communication should be established, it may be necessary to cut through words and other defensive activities and to help the participants become aware of their real response toward each other again through the use of feelings in their whole body."[12]

---

[11]*Ibid.*, p. 51.
[12]*Joy*, pp. 140–41.

Schutz then proceeds to cite an example as to how this can be done:

> The two persons involved are asked to stand at opposite ends of the room. They are instructed to remain silent, look into each other's eyes, and walk very slowly toward each other. Without planning anything, when the two people get close to each other, they are to do whatever they are impelled from within themselves to do. They are to continue the encounter for as long as they wish. After it is completed the principals will ordinarily talk about their feelings, and the others will contribute their observations and identifications with the principals. It is essential to urge the principals to try to let their feelings take over and not plan what they will do when they meet. (Try it now before reading on if you have a companion.) Many variations appear and should be noted, such as which person wants to leave first, how uncomfortable each feels, if they embrace whether it is a warm feeling or a way of avoiding looking at each other, who initiates the action, and so on.[13]

The following example illustrates this particular kind of encounter:

> George had just been divorced and had a great deal of hostility as well as a great attraction toward women. However his feelings toward women were confused, and he treated the whole area rather flippantly and with many jokes. Marla was a very attractive

[13] *Ibid.*, p. 141.

woman, but had very ambivalent feelings toward men.

She was very dependent on them on the one hand, and very competitive on the other. She and George had avoided each other in the group until someone remarked that their feelings toward the opposite sex seemed similar and wondered how they felt about each other. Characteristically neither would identify or verbalize how they actually felt toward the other. They said that they did not feel anything. It seemed like an appropriate time for an encounter since it might allow them to become aware of their feelings toward each other that were being blocked inside them. They approached each other slowly and when they met, George looked at Marla briefly and walked right by her, staring straight ahead. For fully five minutes both stood still, backs to each other, looking in opposite directions. The tension became too great for the observers and they began to urge the principals on to various solutions of the impasse, but George and Marla accepted none. Then Marla stepped back, took George by the shoulders and turned him around so that she was facing his back. She then stepped back and the group waited anxiously for the next move. They did not have to wait long, for Marla stepped up and delivered a tremendous kick in the rear to George, knocking him several feet across the room. Stunned, George looked at Marla, who then invited him to kick her back. He refused until she finally took a pillow and put it behind her. Reluctantly, George kicked her, but gently. The effect of this interchange was different for the two participants. Marla felt elated and strong, her participation in

> the group increased, and she became softer. Later, in a psychodrama, she was able to work on her relation to her father, which helped her clarify her feelings toward men. George became depressed. His difficulties with women were serious and he was forced to face them directly, something he had successfully avoided up to that time.
>
> In effect the encounter allowed Marla to experience one of her most basic fears, male rejection, blatant and unmistakable—a man looked at her, walked away, and turned his back. She found strength to deal with the situation however, by expressing the anger and hurt most directly, and then being able to show compassion and fairness. She had coped successfully with a very frightening situation and felt the exhilaration of her success. The softness felt later was the femininity that could come through now that men did not have to be attacked out of her fear of being rejected by them. For George, the encounter confronted him starkly with the severity of his problem and tore away his frivolous exterior. He could not feel much for a woman, and what he did feel was anger. He could not fake jocular feelings in the encounter, and he was forced to feel—literally—the effect of his behavior on the woman.

Schutz relates that in subsquent meetings he settled down to working on the problem. What happened in both cases was that the encounter stripped away the verbalization and presented the problem in its most basic terms, allowing in one case a partial solution and in the other a more realistic inspection.

We all know that traditional psychoanalysis does not encourage acting out, but in a sense the acting out which takes place in the groups at Esalen as directed by Perls and Schutz do benefit the patient. There is a minimum of interpretation but an emphasis on getting to your feelings. A former patient of mine, Frank, discovered that when he, upon my advice, visited Esalen. One of Frank's problems all along had been that he *could not feel* and it sometimes was difficult for me, existential as I am with my patients, to establish contact and communication with him. He had been terribly emotionally deprived. His parents were cold fish and devoid of any feeling toward each other and toward Allan. The pathology as a result was severe, his sexual identity was confused, and he was totally unable to function with other people. He had to force himself to stay at the job that he was doing and always felt a terrible pressure upon him. He never could relax, either laugh or cry, for that matter.

Although I had gone as far as I could possibly go in what could be described as an existential psychoanalytic situation, I felt that he needed something else in therapy that I could not possibly provide. At that time Esalen was written up, and I asked him if he were interested in going out there. During his summer vacation (he was a high school teacher) he went out to California. Upon his return I asked him to write down his experiences and here are some of his rather moving impressions,

> This woman about forty and a child psychologist began to talk about herself. She went around the room telling everybody how stupid she really was, debasing herself and that way of feeling that she really was not so bad. But she wanted to do that. Well, I felt she was taking too much time and I said you know you are really dominating this situa-

tion, you are taking too much time and she said, well what do you want to do? What do you want to do? And I said I want everybody to tell me how stupid I am. She said okay, lay down on the floor, and everybody else got in a circle around me and kept telling me how stupid I was. So they were in this circle above me and they were saying, "You are stupid, you are stupid, Frank, you know that, you are stupid." And I was telling them I know you are right! I am really stupid, I live my life stupidly, now I expect to start saying yeah, I am an idiot, like I am not smart at all I cannot. . . . But I did not say this, I said "I am stupid I do not live my life intelligently, I live my life like an idiot, everything I do is just . . . like I do not know it does not make sense, but I got to live my life. And I just fuck it up and I know better and I do it so stupidly, there is no reason for it." And then I started to cry. I had not cried about problems that affected me in I think ten to fifteen years. "I cry at movies, maybe I shed a tear at—and you know you are right. I am really stupid, you know I live life stupidly." Now I expected to start saying something like "Yeah I am an idiot, I am stupid, I am not smart at all." But I did not say that, I said, "No I am stupid because I do not live my life intelligently. I live my life like an idiot. Everything I do is just . . . Like I know it does not make sense . . . There is just no reason for it." And I started to cry again. When I cry, I cry at movies or at a sentimental part of a book. But that is not me, that is something that happens to other people. What happens to me never seems to really hit me. Very rarely. And suddenly there I was crying and the leader told me to stand up. I felt so lonely, and so bad about my life. And he told everyone to hold me. And everyone held me. I felt sort of good about that. I wanted to keep this feeling of sadness and crying. I wanted to burden myself into myself and I wanted nothing else but live my life sensibly and real. I was losing the feeling of sadness, but still had the feeling how deeply I had hurt myself. And how lonely I was. And then I started to sing, to recapture, I started to sing a song called . . . well, it is a song from *The Graduate* and says, "Hello, darkness, my friend, I'll be with you till the end." These are not the exact words but those are the words that I sort of made up about darkness. "Hello, darkness, my old friend, I'll be with you till the end." And I started crying again. And some of them sang it along with me. And that is all I kept singing and I laid down on the floor again and they gathered around me and they started to bring me out of it. One of the girls said, "What are you going to do about?" "Are you going to be this way?" And I said, "NO. I have got to change it. I do not want to be this way." And one of the girls said, "Well, how are you going to change it? "You got to fight for the things you want." And I said, "I do not want to be lonely anymore. I want to build a life around me." And the leader said, "Get up, Frank. Now you are on *your* ship. You are the captain of the ship and there is only one life preserver left and the ship is going down. What are you going to do?" And he threw me a pillow (life preserver). And I said, "Well, crew, I'm the captain, and you know the captain is supposed to go down with his ship, but I do not believe in rules and I am not going down

> with my ship, and I am keeping this life preserver and you can go all to hell." So they started all to run and attack me to get the life preserver (the pillow) in order to get it away from me. And I was fighting for it and I really enjoy a fight. I was throwing the pillow right and left and some other people joined in and tried to get it away from me. And I was really doing a great job, really proud of myself . . ."

What is outstanding in all of these experiences is the attempt of the Esalen therapists to get their patients to react to their feelings in a here-and-now situation. The devices used in order to attain such a connection are different. Psychodrama, relaxation exercises, touching and the de-emphasis on the taking of one's life history, all play a role in this process and all contribute to a situation in which the patient is able to deal with some of his problems in a very immediate manner. Obvious is that the Esalen approach has veered away most decisively from a verbal orientation in psychotherapy to a more distinct nonverbal approach. Bernard Gunther, one of the therapists at Esalen writes in his book *Sense Relaxation:*

> Words ultimately become hypnotic conditioning, a series of expectations, leaving little possibility for the excitement of what might be or really is. This is not to condemn language which when accompanied by feeling can be extremely exciting, powerful, delighting, creative, communicative tool, but only to recognize the imbalance that our society has produced. Talking and thinking have become compulsive in many instances; a defense against experience and the world.

> . . . Sensory Awakening is de-hypnosis, a way out of rigid rules, feelings, thoughts, constrictions: being tightly bound. An active meditation: experiments, exercises, and games designed to quiet the overdominant verbal preoccupation of the mind, to let go of chronic excessive muscular tension and focus consciousness on direct sensory experience in the here and now.[14]

Another personal experience on how one experiences the sensory awakening process is recorded by Rasa Gustiatis,

> Farther down on the large lawn (at Esalen) Bernie Gunther has gathered a group of family therapists for a sensory awakening session . . . . I join them. We spread bed sheets on the grass, and lie down on them, closing our eyes. Gunther's voice takes me through my body: feel in contact with the ground, feel how the head touches, the toes, the fingernails. Without moving, travel through yourself with your mind. My right eyelid is burning in the sun, the left one is cool. My head lies heavy and hard, my body is stiff. But I'm aware of the supple grass beneath the sheet. Now stand up and tap with fingers, loose-wristed, all over the head. Pleasurable whiteness sinks in under closed eyes. Open the eyes. Slap your forehead, jaw, lips, cheeks, tap softly with fingertips on the closed lids. Feel the face loosen and a tingling sensation spread through the head. Take a partner, look at him. I see a man with eyelid twitching, mouth stiff in self-conscious-

---

[14]Bernard Gunther, *Sense Relaxation* (New York; Collier Books, 1968), pp. 59, 89.

> ness. He arouses my sympathy, I tap his head, then look into his face. He twitches less now. Good. We smile briefly, pass on to new partners. Gunther . . . aims to tune people in to their senses. His method is adapted mainly from the work by Charlotte Selver. He also uses techniques derived from his study of Gestalt therapy, Zen, yoga and massage.[15]

In reviewing some of the Esalen techniques we are struck by the fact that so much of what goes on at Esalen is based on the principles of Gestalt therapy. What comes through in all the therapeutic experiences at Esalen is the stress of the *now* and its aim to get the patient in touch with his feelings at once. The idea of the *now*, of the immediate moment, of the content and structure of present experience is one of the most potent principles of Gestalt therapy. In order to promote the *now* awareness the Gestalt therapists at Esalen and elsewhere encourage communications in the present tense. What is your present awareness? What is happening now? What do you feel at this moment? Thus there is a tendency to de-emphasize historical material, and when this material does appear it is dealt with actively when the Gestalt therapist feels that it is germane to important themes of the present personality structure. This means that the most effective means of integrating past material into the personality is to bring it as soon as possible to the present. It is pointed out to the patient how easily he leaves the now. There is a need of all patients to bring into dialogue absent individuals, the nostalgic urge to reminisce, the tendency to become preoccupied with fears and fan-

[15]*Turning On*, p. 57.

tasies of the future, all of these have to be identified for the patient.

There is a tremendous emphasis at Esalen (and in general among the encounter groups) to change the "It" to "I." Instead of "It is trembling," "*I* am trembling." Rather than "It is choked," "I am choked." And even going one step further, rather than "I am choked," "I am choking myself." The Gestalt therapists maintain that there is a real distinction between "I feel choked" and "I am choking myself," in terms of the different degree of responsibility and involvement that is experienced. Changing "it" to "I" is an example in microcosm of many of the Gestalt techniques. As the patient participates in this particular game—as the Gestaltists prefer to call it—he is far more likely to see himself as an active agent who does things rather than a passive creature to whom things somehow "happen."

As an example of such a game we present the following:

Patient: I can't do that.

Analyst: Can you say, "I won't do that?"

As the patient accepts and uses the analyst's formulation, the analyst commonly follows with ". . . and what do you experience now?" Or . . .

Analyst: What do you hear in your voice?

Patient: My voice sounds it is crying.

Analyst: Can you take responsibility for that by saying, "I am crying?"

Another technique used in the Esalen groups is the awareness continuum. The following exchange illustrates this:

Analyst: What are you aware of now?

Patient: Now I am aware of talking to you. I see others in the room. I'm aware of John squirming. I can feel the tension in my shoulders. I'm aware that I get anxious as I say this.

Analyst: How do you experience the anxiety?

Patient: I hear my voice quiver. My mouth feels dry. I talk in a very halting way.

Analyst: Are you aware of what your eyes are doing?

Patient: Well, now I realize that my eyes keep looking away.

Analyst: Can you take responsibility for that?

Patient: . . . that I keep looking away from you.

Analyst: Can you *be* your eyes now? Write the dialogue for them.

Patient: I am Mary's eyes. I find it hard to gaze steadily. I keep jumping and darting about . . .

The awareness continuum has inexhaustible applications for the Gestalt therapists. Primarily, however, it is an effective way of guiding the individual to the firm bedrock of his experiences and away from endless, thin verbalizations, explanations, speculations, interpretations. Awareness of body feelings (as illustrated by Bernard Gunther at Esalen), of sensations and perceptions, constitutes the most certain knowledge for the Gestalt therapist. They implement Perls's dictum, "lose your mind and come to your senses."

As the Gestalt therapist helps the patient to rely on his senses ("return to his senses") they also help him to distinguish between the reality *out there* and the frightening goblins he manufactures in his own fantasies.

Patient: I'm sure people will despise me for what I just said.

Analyst: Go around the room and look at us careful-

ly. Tell me what you SEE, what your eyes—not your imaginings—tell you.
Patient: Well, actually people don't *look* so rejecting. Some of you even look warm and friendly.
Analyst: What do you experience now?
Patient: I'm more relaxed now.

As in many of the Gestalt techniques there is a no-gossiping rule, which rule is designed to promote feelings and to prevent *avoidance* of feelings. Gossiping in the Gestalt techniques is defined as talking about an individual when he is actually present and could just as well be addressed directly.
Let us say that the analyst is dealing with Bill and Ann in the group:

Bill: (to the analyst) . . . the trouble with Ann is she's always picking on me.
Analyst: You're gossiping; say this to Ann.
Bill (turning to Ann): You're always picking on me.

It is true that we often gossip about people when we have not been able to handle directly the *feelings* they have aroused in us. The no-gossiping rule in the Gestalt therapeutic situation thus facilitates a direct confrontation of feelings.

The idea and concept of confrontation is a recurrent factor in the Gestalt therapy approach. This occurs for example when the therapist asks the patient to *make the rounds.* The analyst may feel that a particular theme or feeling expressed by the patient should be faced vis-à-vis every other person in the group. The patient may have said, "I can't stand anyone in this room." The analyst will then say "Okay, make the rounds. Say that to each one of us and add some other remark pertaining to your feelings about each person." There are of course many variations on this theme and in the Esalen context it may involve touching, caressing, observing, frightening, and so forth.

One way the Gestalt therapist approaches certain symptoms or difficulties is to help the patient realize that the overt behavior will commonly represent the reversal of underlying or latent impulses. Therefore he often uses the reversal technique. For example, the patient claims to suffer from inhibition or excessive timidity. He is asked to play the part of an exhibitionist. In taking this plunge into an area fraught with anxiety he makes contact with a part of himself that has long been submerged. The patient for that matter might be unassertive and overly sweet. He then may be asked to play the part of an uncooperative and spiteful person.

One of the most frequent principles in the Gestalt therapeutic approach is "Can you stay with this feeling?" This technique is invoked at key moments when the patient refers to a feeling or mood or state of mind which is unpleasant and which he has a great urge to dispel. For example, he might have arrived at a point where he feels empty or confused or frustrated or discouraged. The therapist will say, "Can you stay with this feeling?" This inevitably is always a dramatic moment and a frustrating one for the patient. He has referred to his experience with some sourness and is obviously impatient to get it done with, i.e., to leave the feeling behind him. The analyst becomes almost cold-blooded and asks the patient to deliberately remain with whatever psychic pain he has at that moment.

In a sense the Gestalt therapist at this moment is falling back on the awareness continuum. The patient is asked to elaborate on the "what" and "how" of his experience. What are your sensations, perceptions, fantasies and expectancies?

The "stay with it" technique illustrates par excellence Fritz Perls's emphasis on the role of phobic avoidance in all neurotic behavior. In his view, the neurotic has habitually avoided vigorous contact with a variety of unpleasant and dysphoric experiences. As a result, avoidance has become ingrained (a mechanism, so to say), a phobic type of anxiety has been routinized, and major dimensions of experience have never been adequately mastered. Someone reminded me that the title of Fritz Perls's first book is *Ego, Hunger, and Aggression*, and the basic message of that title evidently is that we must adopt toward psychological and emotional experiences the same *active*, coping attitudes that we employ in healthy eating. In healthy eating we bite the food, then we effectively chew, grind, and liquefy the food. Now it can be swallowed, digested, metabolized and assimilated.

The Gestalt therapist, most especially with the "stay with it" technique, encourages the patient to undertake a similar "chewing up" and painstaking assimilation of emotional experiences that have hitherto been unpleasant to the taste, difficult to swallow and impossible to digest. In this way, the patient moves towards improved self-confidence and a greater capacity for autonomy.

Before evaluating the Esalen and Gestalt experiences I want to return once more to Fritz Perls:

> These are the two legs upon which Gestalt Therapy walks: *now* and *how*. The essence of the theory of Gestalt Therapy is in the understanding of these two words. *Now* covers all that exists. The past is no more, the

> future is not yet. *Now* includes the balance of being here, is experiencing, involvement, phenomenon, awareness. *How* covers everything that is structure, behavior, all that is actually going on—the ongoing process. All the rest is irrelevant—computing, apprehending, and so on.[16]

In the end Perls defines and analyzes the *healthy* person in the following terms:

> An absolutely healthy person is completely in touch with himself and with reality. The crazy person, the psychotic, is more or less completely *out* of touch with both, but mostly with *either* himself *or* the world. We are in between being psychotic and being healthy, and this is based upon the fact that we have *two* levels of existence. One is reality, the actual, realistic level, that we are in touch with whatever goes on now, in touch with our feelings, in touch with our senses. Reality is awareness of ongoing experience, actual touching, seeing, moving, doing. The other level we don't have a good word for, so I choose the Indian word *maya*. *Maya* means something like illusion, or fantasy, or philosophically speaking, the *as if* of Vaihinger. *Maya* is a kind of dream, a kind of trance. Very often this fantasy, this *maya*, is called the mind, but if you look a bit closer, what you call "mind" is fantasy. It's the rehearsal stage. Freud once said: "*Denken ist prober arbeit*"—thinking is rehearsing, trying out. Unfortunately, Freud never followed up this discovery because it would have been inconsistent with his genetic approach. If he had

---

[16]*Gestalt Therapy Verbatum*, p. 44.

> accepted his statement, "Thinking is rehearsing," he would have realized how our fantasy activity is turned toward the future, because we rehearse for the future.[17]

It is also interesting to note sensitivity training became an important element in the Esalen approach. Actually the term sensitivity training is used loosely to include a wide range of laboratory-training approaches in human relations, group dynamics, organizational development, as well as a number of verbal and nonverbal experiences that seek to increase awareness and release human potential. In all fairness it should be said that it was neither the author of *Joy*, Bill Schutz, nor the devoted creators of Esalen who were responsible for the development of human relations training. Rather, it was Leland Bradford, then Director of the Adult Education Division of the National Education Association, together with Ronald Lippitt of the University of Michigan and my old friend Kenneth Benne, now of the Boston University Human Relations Center, who were primarily responsible. They drew mainly on the work of famous social psychologist Kurt Lewin and established the first training center more than two decades ago at Bethel, Maine and founded the National Training Laboratories.

As the field developed, the T-group (Training group) became the heart of any laboratory or workshop that is devoted to the study of group dynamics or human relations. The traditional T-group consists of a small group of people—ideally ten to sixteen—who meet in a residential setting (the laboratory) for approximately two weeks. Although only one part of this educational experience (theory, interpretation,

---

[17] *Ibid.*, pp. 46–47.

and skill development are also included), the T-group is, because of its intense emotional impact, by far the most significant aspect of any human relations lab. The objectives of the T-group are to help the individual participants become aware of why both they and others behave as they do in groups—or, become aware of the underlying behavior dynamics of the group. This is accomplished, with the help of a trainer, by creating an atmosphere in which the motivations for typical human behavior, of which individuals are often unaware, are brought to the surface in an exaggerated form. Once they are made clear and explicit, they can be discussed and analyzed. Thus, the individual participant can observe both his own behavior and that of others in the group, discover sources of different kinds of behavior, and identify the effect they have upon the functioning of the group. The effort to stimulate exaggerated behavior in order to get at the motivation behind it more explicitly is an uncomfortable experience for many people, but the feeling is usually transitory. The emotional component of the experience makes it appear to verge on therapy, but there is a significant difference between therapy that is focused on the problems of emotionally disturbed people and training that aims at the improvement of human relations skills of normal people.

In the early years of the movement, the T-group emphasis was primarily on the sociology of groups rather than on their psychology—that is, on the roles and functions of leadership and membership, rather than on the individual personality and personal development. The trend toward a psychological emphasis appeared in the early 1950s when the movement began to attract a larger number of people trained in clinical psychology or psychiatry. (Hence its relationships with the new encounter groups and the Esalen groups.) It was at this point that the T-group emerged as a new social invention that bears some rough resemblance to a combination of seminar and therapy groups.

In the link between Esalen, Gestalt therapy and the T-groups (sensitivity training) I think it is important to realize that encounter groups, confrontation sessions and marathon labs were very much a part of the T-group approach. All of these experiences are usually short-term—most often twenty-four hours or a weekend—experiences where its emphasis is on the direct exposure of beliefs and feelings that usually are not put on public display by individuals.

It should be noted that the term "encounter group" derives from the phrase "basic encounter group" that Carl Rogers, the noted exponent of nondirective counseling, coined to differentiate a new kind of experience from the traditional T-group. Trainers in these sessions usually encourage participants to explore in some depth their own feelings and motivations, as well those of other group members. The objective is to stimulate an exchange that is inhibited by a minimum of reserve and defensiveness in order to achieve a maximum of openness and honesty.

The sensitivity people also believe in the so-called confrontation sessions, which are usually contrived racial encounters in which militant blacks literally confront members of the white community with their angry reaction to white racism, discrimination and prejudice. Since most confrontation sessions of this kind are not part of a plan for organizational change, they usually end as paratherapeutic experiences rather than training.

The nonverbal exercises, which play an important part in the Esalen experience, have invaded the training field with a vengeance in recent years. The techniques employed are numerous and range from simple exercises with a minimum of body contact to physically intimate and emotionally revealing designs of the kind most often associated with Esalen and other institutes. The value of nonverbal techniques cannot be underestimated, they derive their theoretical justification from theories of personality that stress the possibility of achieving greater honesty and authenticity through bodily expression that can become uninhibited more quickly than can verbal communication.

In evaluating the Esalen experience we are struck by the fact that so much of what is going on at Esalen relates to the crisis of the individual in this society. There is no doubt that the great problem *now* at *this* point in *this society* is the absence of feelings among many, either young or old. The detachment, the coldness, the absence of human feelings are, to our distress, very relevant to many people in our society today. It seems to me that with all the shortcomings of the Esalen approach it has at least reestablished the significance of human feelings in the here-and-now situation. It does not take *no* for an answer, it does not fool around with a polite evasiveness, it tries to confront people (how few it might be) with their feelings. Somehow such an approach goes beyond therapy and I am sure that Perls and others are aware of that.

It is one of the achievements of Perls and Schutz that they have brought therapy back to life once again, that they are refusing to follow the orthodox, safe path, that they are willing and prepared to take risks to bring their patients back to the world in which they did not have a place left. Certainly they do not make it easy for their patients. They require hard work and devotion, but at the same time they also are compassionate in their approach. Sure, they do fail, but they do not fail out of their own inadequacies, I am sure, but much more because they are dealing with such a wide variety of patients, who do present themselves upon their doorsteps with a sense of urgency and expectation.

I have a great respect for those in the therapeutic field who are willing to take risks and are not just content with their routine practice but are enough in touch to notice that other methods and techniques perhaps are required *now* to deal with new patients and new problems. One of the assets of Perls (and, by implication, Esalen) is that he has cut through many of our orthodox pretenses, and I quote him as a close to this chapter:

> Any time you use the words *now* and *how*, and become aware of this, you grow. Each time you use the question *why*, you diminish in stature. You bother yourself with false, unnecessary information. You only feed the computer, the intellect. And the intellect is the whore of intelligence. It's a drag on your life.[18]

[18]*Ibid.*

THE BIOENERGETIC AND PHYSICALLY ORIENTED GROUPS

If there ever was a taboo in traditional psychoanalysis it certainly was the taboo of touch. Most orthodox psychoanalysts do not even shake hands with their patients, let alone consider any kind of physical interaction with their patients. Indeed, classical psychoanalytic technique imposes one definite taboo: patient and analyst may not touch each other.[1] To violate this rule, Karl Menninger holds, gives "evidence of the incompetence or criminal ruthlessness of the analyst."[2]

[1]Elizabeth Mintz, "Touch and the Psychoanalytic Tradition" (unpublished paper).

[2]Karl Menninger, *Theory of Psychoanalytic Technique* (New York: Basic Books, 1958), p. 40.

Although this taboo has slightly eroded during the past decade, especially in the context of individual psychotherapy, there are still many psychotherapists who feel very dubious, to say the least, about physical contact in the psychoanalytic situation.

In the discussion about the employment of physical touch in psychotherapy there is an important sociological consideration, which should be talked about. Unlike people in Europe, Americans feel very awkward about touching other people. Men are literally terrified of touching other men, even in the context of camaraderie, since any physical expression of affection might be interpreted as latent or overt homosexuality. It is very seldom that one notices physical affection between American males. On the contrary, they shy away from it. We should emphasize that this does not apply only to physical affection between males, physical affection and touch are to a large extent taboo in American society.* The absence of physical touch and affection among American people, has in my opinion, contributed significantly to the estrangement and alienation of the 1950s and 1960s. The complaints about an absence of intimacy among many people in our society is only a part of the picture of our contemporary patient and of the average American today.

The fear of physical touch, affection and intimacy has of course a great deal to do with the phenomenon of Americans to verbalize their intimate feelings rather than to express them. It is easy to get any

---

*I happened to grow up in Holland and I remember distinctly that even as a boy of twelve I would walk arm in arm with my father. Such was not at all unusual and it is an illustration of the fact that physical affection and touch was (and is) much more incorporated into the social structure of European society.

American to talk about his problems and intimate matters concerning himself and his family, but he shies away from the human expression of affection and touch. Part of this, especially in terms of the males, has of course to do with the notion that males have to be tough, unsentimental and, God forbid, that they should listen to classical music!* Unfortunately there still seems to be a prototype of an American male, and we all know that contemporary politicians like former President Johnson and Vice-President Agnew do not help matters by talking about "nervous Nellies" and "impudent and effete snobs." Such statements are only a testimony to the fact that this society where it concerns masculinity, one's manly performance and the whole area of physicality and intimacy, is still raw and primitive. This is all coupled with the so-called American myth that one has to be strong and tough in all one's actions. No wonder that contemporary individual and group psychotherapies found such a fertile ground for their notion that people should start expressing their feelings, emotions and their repressed desires for physical affection and touch.

I feel that somewhere along the line, especially in terms of contemporary American child-rearing, some fundamental notions about the importance of warmth, affection, touch and being close to another human being have been lost or ignored. No matter how many of our child-rearing experts have told us how to rear the children, there seems to be a flaw in all of it. Numerous young patients, from all ethnic groups, have confirmed to me that physical affection was almost totally absent in their growing-up years.

---

*I recently read that Joseph Kennedy, Sr., liked classical music, but did not want his friends to know, since it might be considered effeminate!

And are those young people not precisely the people who are now participating in the Esalen experience or in the various sensitivity training programs? Since American child-rearing has been pretty much *programmed* during the last decades it might be that such important aspects like affection and touch have been programmed out of their experience!

One is almost surprised about the reaction of many people to the introduction of touch and physicality into the contemporary encounter groups. Touch is by now considered something totally new in the experience of many people either in or outside therapy. It seems to me a sad illustration of the plight of the alienated and lonely person in our midst today that the mere introduction of touch almost signifies a revolution of sorts.

In the last decade when the need for new ways and innovations in psychotherapy became quite urgent the question of touch in the therapeutic process again was revived. Although probably in the inner sanctum of the psychoanalyst's office more touch had taken place (more than the orthodox analyst would like to admit) than we realized, the issue of touch became relevant in the emergence of the new group and individual therapies. Many therapists felt that in an anxiety-ridden and self-estranged society like ours we simply could not uphold the same kind of standards as in nineteenth century Vienna. And they had (and have) a point, since the type of patient seen by early analysts was not deprived of physical affection and warmth. The setup of the traditional family took care of that. With the increase in borderline cases, a definite increase in schizophrenia—an obvious detachment from the world—other techniques and, more important, another *philosophy* of psychoanalysis were called for.

In the employment of touch in the new group therapies a distinction should be made between touch as part of a spontaneous gesture, the desire to illustrate the closeness in a given psychoanalytic situation by physical touch, and the kind of touch that is employed by the neo-Reichians, such as Alexander Lowen in his bioenergetic group therapy.

The use of physical touch in the encounter and marathon groups is in my opinion much closer to the sociological reality of this society, which for a long time put a taboo or *Verboten* on the employment of physical touch. One of the liberating aspects of the encounter and marathon groups is that physical touch is being explored in quite a spontaneous and uninhibited manner. People who are uptight and rigid in their encounters and interaction with others might derive quite a relief from the use of physical touch. It also might be quite a comfort to those who were deprived in childhood and adolescence of physical touch. Thus the use of physical touch in such situations becomes almost a learning process. Something is discovered (or perhaps rediscovered) and enjoyed. In the encounter, marathon and sensitivity groups such physical encounter might have quite a significance for the individuals involved. It might break age-old barriers of taboo and prejudice, and it offers the participants a real alternative to being rigid and uptight.

The appearance of physical touch in the marathon and encounter groups is closely linked to the concept and phenomenon of spontaneity. The lack of spontaneity in contemporary, alienated people inhibits them in expressing their emotions and feelings, including the desire to express those feelings in a physical manner. Thus if we revive spontaneity in the encounter meetings, we also open up possibilities and opportunities for physical expression simply as an illustration of "feeling good" about a person in the group. Such a situation is of course not structured and it depends entirely on the course a given marathon or encounter group will take if such physical expression is to take place.

I think it is important to stress the link between spontaneity and physical touch (or expression) in this particular analytic situation since the nature of the encounter group calls for a commitment on the part of the individuals involved to place themselves on the line (or, spot) and really express their feelings in the here-and-now situation. If sponotaneity is stressed there can be no inhibitions about what one wants to express, and so any kind of physical closeness will be appropriate in such a situation.

Two analysts can be considered pioneers in the relationship between body and mind in contemporary psychotherapy. The first, and the more well known of the two, is Wilhelm Reich[3] and the second one, still alive and active, is Alexander Lowen.[4] Reich began working in the conventional manner, around the 1920s, analyzing patients' resistances and being a part of the conventional psychoanalytic es-

---

[3]For more data on Reich's life see his last wife's biography of Reich: Ilse Ollendorff Reich, *Wilhelm Reich* (New York: St. Martin's Press, 1969, Avon, 1970), and also Mary Higgins and Chester M. Raphael, *Reich Speaks of Freud* (New York: Farrar, Straus, & Giroux, 1967); Michal Cattier, *La Vie et L'Oeuvre du Docteur Wilhelm Reich* (Paris, La Cite, N.Y.); J. M. Palmier, *Wilhelm Reich* (Paris: Le Monde en 1018, 1969). Two outstanding books of Reich: *Character Analysis* (New York: Noonday Press, 1967) and *The Function of the Orgasm* (New York: Bantam Books, 1967).

[4]Of the works by Alexander Lowen, see especially his *Physical Dynamics of Character Structure* (New York: Grune & Stratton, 1958) and *The Betrayal of the Body* (New York: Macmillan, 1967).

tablishment. For years he was a member of the Viennese Psychoanalytic Society, knew Freud well, and was married to an orthodox Freudian psychoanalyst, Annie Reich, whom he later divorced. Soon he found that it was *character resistance*, the patient's attitude and bearing—mental and physical—that offered crucial material. Patients developed this "characterological armor" in order to conceal aspects of their past, information that was vital to success in treatment.

Later Reich came to think that disturbances in psychological character and peculiarities of muscular posture served the same function: each tended to divert or economize psychic energy; muscular tension and emotional block were equivalent. And, since they were equivalent, the psychotherapist could legitimately attack either as a means toward learning about the patient's problems and helping him to resolve them.

The therapist now had two instruments. If psychic influence through free association, say, did not seem to affect a patient's resistance, then work on a bodily posture or gesture might be more successful. A patient of Reich expressed his character resistance by talking a great deal and, especially, by gossiping about acquaintances in his analytic sessions. Yet, often, he seemed to finger his mouth as if to reassure himself that it was there. For this patient revealed, finally, his feeling that his mouth did not belong to him; it was "dead," an alien thing.

Reich's patient showed a change, the loss of this defensiveness, when his mouth curled into an infantile sucking shape although, during the same session, the patient would have a hard, mean expression on his face.

The therapist touched the man's neck, one day, merely to see whether the muscles were unusually tense. To Reich's surprise, "the patient immediately assumed the attitude of a hanged man," head limp, tongue protruded, mouth open. Once a patient, took this posture, he was able to recall and talk about his infantile fear of death, specifically, of being hanged for sinful behavior—masturbation. He did not put on the aspect of a hanged man unless he kept his breathing shallow. When the patient stopped being afraid of breathing deeply, he lost the hanged corpse's attitude—and many of his other problems as well.[5]

Here, difficulty in breathing was a sign of psychological disturbance and return to the ability to breath normally was an indication of returning health. Reichian and neo-Reichian therapists (who accept some of his techniques although they reject much of his theory)[6] accept his emphasis on the link between body and mind. Many conventional psychoanalysts would recognize the existence of the link but regard it as a truism which can contribute nothing to the actual analytic technique. Reich's followers, on the other hand, not only observe the patient's respiration, for example, but seek to correct irregularities and other difficulties. For instance, holding the breath and tightening the belly are frequent indications of effort to suppress anxiety and other unpleasant feelings. Others concentrate on muscular tensions.

Alexander Lowen is a leader among those therapists who regard muscular tension as a basic factor in

---

[5]Reich's *The Function of the Orgasm*, p. 233.

[6]Rejection of Reich's ideas about orgone biophysics has affected the judgment of some contemporary analysts. They do not give Reich's sound analytic approach the regard it deserves because, rightly, they think his later ideas are irrelevant to psychoanalysis.

emotional disturbances and who try to dispel that tension as a means of dealing with the patient's problems. The body, Lowen argues, has one fundamental energy, *bioenergy*, which is manifested by emotions and muscles alike. Every neurotic problem has its bodily counterpart. The schizoid person wears a mask; his fixed smile and knowing look hide the expression of a death's head. When the expression does not appear, the therapist's pressure on the cheekbones will bring it out. "The (schizoid) patient," Lowen writes, "is not aware of this expression . . . but its presence is another gauge to the depth of his fear."[7]

In the work which Lowen and others are doing in the realm of bioenergetic group therapy, it is important to stress the difference between them and the encounter groups in terms of the employment of touch.

First of all bioenergetic therapy is an approach to the problems of the human personality through the direct involvement of the body in the psychanalytic process. The body is involved in three ways: First, it is sufficiently exposed to be available for the interpretation of its expression and the analysis of its form and movement. In the psychoanalytic situation, men wear trunks and women wear leotards or other suitable apparel. Second, the body's energy processes are mobilized through breathing and movement to facilitate the expression of feeling, and a setting is provided for the release of the repressed feelings that become activated in the course of this mobilization. Third, the physical work with the body allows direct physical contact between patient and therapist. The

[7]Alexander Lowen, *The Betrayal of the Body* (New York: Macmillan, 1966), p. 66.

desire for and fear of this contact is one of the main conflicts, according to Lowen, et al., from which all patients suffer.

Lowen states it quite clearly,

> Nakedness is the great leveler of social distinctions for it reduces all persons to the common bodily or animal level on which they came into this world. Nudity strips the individual of his ego pretensions and, sometimes, of his ego defenses. Punishment has frequently taken the form of the public exposure of the naked body. People who are paraded nude through the streets before the gaze of others who are dressed experience a deep humiliation. When, however, everyone is undressed, the feelings of shame and embarrassment tend to disappear and one often experiences a sense of release and freedom in nudity. The need to maintain an appearance or support an ego image is a restraint that inhibits the joy and spontaneity of the body. In the privacy of our homes, we all welcome the opportunity to relieve ourselves of this ego burden by removing some of our clothing.[8]

Alexander Lowen stresses the close relationship between body and mind:

> " . . . the body is the person, the person is his body. We have no real existence apart from our bodies. What goes on in our minds is, basically, a reflection of what goes on in our bodies. Whether a person is a "somebody" or a "nobody" must depend funda-

---

[8]Alexander Lowen, "In Defense of Modesty," *The Journal of Sex Research,* Vol. 1, IV, No. 1 (February, 1968), p. 52.

> mentally upon the quality of his bodily function. If a person's body is vibrant and alive, he will impress us accordingly and we will relate to him differently from the way we would relate to a person whose body is relatively lifeless in its expression. Our intuitive response to a person is determined by how we sense his bodily qualities. The look in a person's eyes, the tone of his voice, the expression of his mouth, the warmth of his handshake, the way he carries himself, and the degree of his vivacity and spontaneity are not only signs that tell us who he is; they are the factors that determine our unconscious or feeling reaction to him.[9]

In the bioenergetic groups the total body picture is studied from two views. One is the form or shape of the body, and the other is the degree of flexibility or rigidity of the body. It requires considerable skill, which should be stressed here, and experience to interpret a body picture accurately, but a group is always more perceptive in doing so than a single person.* In examining the form of the body as each member stands before the group, the members look at proportion, harmony, facial expression, posture, etc. Does a person stand firmly on his feet or does he seem suspended from his shoulders? Is he too thin or too fat, too muscular or asthenic? Does the person stand erect or with bowed head and hunched shoulders? Are the hips too heavy or the shoulders too broad? Finally, each member of the group usually is asked to describe his impression of the person standing before him. The discussion that follows provides

---

[9]Alexander Lowen, "Bio-energetic Group Therapy," in Hendrik M. Ruitenbeek, ed., *Group Therapy Today.*

*In all groups patients function as therapists!

an opportunity for each person present to develop his understanding of body language.

This understanding of the body language is crucial to the bioenergetic group therapy and Lowen cites the following example:

> In a group I conducted some years ago an astute observation by one of the members deepened my own understanding of this language. The person under observation presented an interesting picture. He was a man about fifty, with a large head, a short neck, and a heavy, solid body. His eyes were small, his mouth had a somewhat cynical expression, and his jaw was set and hard. He used a characteristic phrase with which the group had gained some familiarity in the course of its meetings. It was, "I couldn't care less." Among his other problems, this man was an alcoholic. The surprising thing about his body was the seeming lack of support by his legs. His feet were rather small for his size and tightly contracted. His legs were underdeveloped and muscularly and extremely tense. Looking at him, one of the group said, "You lack understanding." To appreciate this comment, the term *understanding* must be contrasted with ego-standing. This person held a significant ego position in the community. He came from a wealthy family, was the head of an important business, owned a fine home, and so on. The personal base for this position was weak and insecure as reflected by alcoholism, marital discord, and other difficulties. The biological base, namely the feeling of having his legs under him, his feet well planted and balanced on the ground, was equally weak. Committed in the upper half of his body to

> an imposing ego image, this man lacked both a physical understanding of his personality and a psychological understanding of his problems.[10]

Since we have come to realize how important *feelings* are in the process of group therapy it seems interesting to note that the bioenergetic approach tries to combine the feeling-tone on the patient and his muscular tensions. Bioenergetic group therapy provides the techniques whereby the muscular tensions can be reduced through the mobilization and release of feeling. To understand these techniques one must know that every chronic muscular tension inhibits an impulse. Feelings are expressed through movement, and every muscular spasm is a barrier that blocks or limits the expression of feeling. By eliminating the tension, according to the bioenergetic therapists, one can release the feeling, or by expressing the feeling one can reduce the tension. Both modalities are part of the bioenergetic approach.

A chronically contracted muscle is in effect saying, "no." It says "no" to the impulse that would emerge if the muscle were free to move. It says "no" to the feeling of love or hate that underlies the impulse. To free the muscle, this unconscious "no" must be transformed into a statement in word and deed.

Lowen relates that in the group session each individual takes his turn in expressing the "no." Lying on a bed with a foam mattress he is asked to strike the bed repeatedly with his fists and say "no" with each blow in a loud and convincing tone. The group watches the performance and comments on the effectiveness of the action and the sound. It is, according

---

[10]See *Group Therapy Today*, p. 282.

to Lowen, amazing how few people can produce an action that is convincing. The blows seem to lack force, the voice betrays a note of fear, hesitation, sadness, etc. At this point the group may encourage the subject to "let go," to pound with all his strength and yell with all his might. If it so happens that this encouragement is ineffectual, the group then may point out his fear of self-assertion. The members of the group may probe his relationship to his parents or may taunt him with a challenge.

Lowen relates that kicking is one of the basic movements of bioenergetic therapy. And he maintains that to kick is to protest, and that every person in our culture has something to protest about. In the bioenergetic group situation feelings of negation and hostility are not directed toward any group member, which is far different from the traditional group where many hostile and negative feelings are projected on each other. The patient in bioenergetic group therapy is asked to express feeling, not "act it out." One pounds the bed or beats the bed, never another person in the group. This control, according to Lowen, allows the therapy to proceed on an analytic basis. And he cites the following example:

> A woman subject is given a tennis racket and directed to beat the bed. While doing this she is asked to make an appropriate verbal statement such as "I hate you," "You bitch," "Son of a bitch," or "I'll kill you." The group, observing the subject's actions, interacts with her in the following ways. One, it encourages her to be more aggressive, to let go, to let it out. Two, it comments on any disparity between the words used and the expression of the subject's face. The words may be hateful while the expression is smiling, or the

facial expression may be one of rage while the words used are relatively mild. Very often some group members can describe the subject's feeling more accurately than she herself senses it.* Three, the group can ask the subject to name the objects of her anger and question her relation to these people. Since parents are the most common objects of repressed anger, this inquiry opens the subject's background to analytic study.

Lowen feels that since the patient (or subject, as he calls him) in the group is in need of help, comfort and warmth, he should also be able to express such feelings in the group. The patient will lie on the bed with knees bent and head back and will extend both arms and implore, "Please help me." The bioenergetic group will sense the genuineness of this request from the tone of voice and the quality of the movement. If it is genuine, someone approaches and will offer his hand, which the patient will take. When such feelings are sincere, Lowen relates, this might constitute a dramatic moment and often some of the participants will burst into tears and embrace one another. This, incidentally, is not far different from the highly charged emotional moments in the encounter groups and marathon experience, where we also find such spontaneous reactions to a given emotional state of a participant. Also, sometimes the subject is directed to call some close person, for example, "Mama," "Dad," or a spouse. Such an appeal, following as it does the expression of negative feelings, often releases the pent-up longing that the subject has repressed.

Lowen also relates the physical experience

*This is even a common phenomenon in orthodox group therapy. (Ruitenbeek) which takes place between the members of the group and between the therapist and the patient. According to him this physical contact takes two forms. The first is the "laying on of hands" to knead and soften areas of chronic spasticity. Lowen uses the term "laying on of hands" deliberately since he feels that far more is involved than simple massage. He views the contact between therapist and patients in terms of the therapist's hands and the patient's body as an opportunity to express feelings of support, help, reassurance and acceptance that transcend words. The second form of physical contact is holding the patient when he is in distress or embracing him when he is joyful.

It should be emphasized here that such expressions of physical comfort are probably often expressed by other than bioenergetic therapists. The only difference between them and Lowen is that Lowen, et al., write about them, whereas many other therapists consider these actions as something between them and their patients and prefer to keep it that way.

In describing the bioenergetic group activities Lowen stresses the point that each member of the group is taught how to recognize the palpate muscular spasticities. He is also taught a few simple procedures for kneading the tight muscles at the back of the neck and the shoulder area. It is often possible with such simple maneuvers to break the grip of a tension headache that is not too severe and to relax the yoke that binds the shoulders. There are a few other simple body techniques to ease back tensions that the bioenergetic group learns to use not only with the other group members but also with their families.

Lowen also stresses that although bioenergetic

group therapy involves the body it does not eliminate the necessity for a group interaction on the verbal level. This may take place as part of the body work or it may occur independently of it. He maintains that bioenergetic therapy is a "double-barreled attack"—physical and verbal.

Lowen feels that the stress on the body is a new aspect in contemporary group therapy and he also feels that the integration of the physical and verbal aspects of therapy develops spontaneously from the need of the moment. He writes:

> In terms of the group experience, working with the body does something extremely satisfying. One member of a group expressed this "something" succinctly. He said, "I am impressed with how likable each member of the group became after the session." This remark followed an all-day session in which each member participated in all aspects of the body work. We all had the same feeling. There was a noticeable change in each person, especially in his relationship to others. Why had they become more likable? I think because they had become more human. They had abandoned their ego positions to relate to each other on the level that all humanity has in common—the human body.[11]

Others have noticed the absence of the body in the experience of individual and group psychotherapy. Burton remarks,

> . . . the body has been strangely missing in psychotherapy and encounter attempts to re-

[11]See *Group Therapy Today*, p. 289.

> turn it to man. Lowen, while not necessarily an exponent of encountering, makes the most eloquent case for the unification of body and mind. It is paradoxical that the physician, who must have a fundamental training in biology, departs from the body when he becomes a psychiatrist, or at least is at a loss which to treat first when he gets his first patient.[12]

It is interesting to note that Burton believes that the encounter groups place high emphasis on the body:

> Encounter . . . gives the body primacy, and most encountering methods, possibly influenced by yoga, find a central position for bodily sensation and feeling. The pristine joy of a unified body, without Christian sin, is a rare experience and one which fulfillment must countenance . . . Increased conscious, sensory, and body awareness, as a form of encounter, is thus designed to return the body to the disembodied psyche, and to make it feel itself more acutely. There is no reason why a bowel movement, or a deferred urination, should not make its contribution to the hegemony of an individual, as it most certainly does in constipation or prostatis.[13]

In the emphasis of the body with the group therapy Lowen is doing he might somewhat *over*emphasize the importance of the body, when he writes that

---

[12]Arthur Burton, ed., *Encounter* (San Francisco: Jossey-Bass, 1969), p. 14.
[13]*Ibid.*, p. 14.

> the group working with the body gains a feeling of unity through the mutal acceptance of each individual's aspiration for freedom, pleasure, and joy. It is not a unity based on the need for support nor on a common effort against an oppressive force. Within such groups rivalries and resentments inevitably develop. This does not happen in bio-energetic group therapy. Out of respect for one's own body, each individual respects the body and therefore the life and uniqueness of every other person....

However I see nothing wrong with rivalries and resentments in a given group, be it encounter or traditional groups, after all such rivalries and resentments are very much a part of the life we are living and it should be expressed and experienced in the group. It is not enough to stress the unity of body and thereby ignore other aspects of what living means to people in our society.

So we are back where we started from; touch and physicality in individual and group psychotherapy are only part of the patient's total existential experience. The value of Lowen's bioenergetic groups and the encounter groups that employ touch and physicality in their sessions is that they essentially bring back to the patient a long-lost desire to express his feelings in a physical way. Anger can be expressed verbally (and most of the time is) but it also can and should be at times expressed physically. So it goes for affection, words are often not enough to express warmth, human consideration and concern, or simple affection, and the body then has to become involved.

Some of the new group encounter experiences have opened up possibilities in that area and have enabled the patient to add yet another dimension to his search for insight and knowledge of his own self.

The concept of touch in group therapy and in the newer forms of group therapy especially has added another factor to the realm of psychotherapy. It really states that in the encounter of human beings, who for some reason or another are brought together to look for answers and insights, *nothing* can be ignored in reaching such goals. The alienation from self and identity, so common and characteristic of our contemporary patients, has also brought home the awareness and realization that we have ignored the physical encounter in group psychotherapy. We are dealing on the whole with many impoverished patients in our contemporary practice, and by that we do not mean materially impoverished, but those who are literally starving for expressed emotions and feelings. For those a real existential encounter has to include the possibility of touch and the growing realization that no separation between body and mind is possible.

THE ADDICTION GROUPS: SYNANON AND DAYTOP

One of the most striking aspects of the new group therapies is their insistence upon total honesty and forthrightness in the group encounter. No rationalizations or intellectualizations are allowed, and the emphasis upon what one's feelings are in the here-and-now situation is stressed. Directness is the word and a great many of the traditional psychoanalytic concepts such as the process of working through have been abandoned in this new group process.

It is perhaps one of the major contributions of the so-called addiction groups that they have stressed this directness and what Abraham Maslow has called "no-crap therapy" and that indeed these groups have broken radically with the traditional psychoanalytic concepts and rules. Says Maslow:

> What I have read about Synanon, as well what I saw last night and this afternoon, suggests that the whole idea that you mustn't say a loud word to anybody because it might traumatize him or hurt him, the idea that people cry easily or crack easily or commit suicide or go crazy if you shout at them—that maybe these ideas are out-dated. The assumption in your groups seems to be, on the contrary, that people are very tough, and not brittle. They can take an awful lot. The best thing to do is get right at them, and not to sneak up on them, or be delicate with them, or try to surround them from the rear. Get right smack into the middle of things right away. I've suggested that a name for this might be "no-crap therapy." It serves to clean out the defenses, the rationalizations, the veils, the evasions and politeness of the world.[1]

Actually Synanon originally was a community of former addicts and criminals founded by Charles Dederich, a former alcoholic in California. The word "synanon" originated with a newly arrived addict in the early days of the organization. In his attempt to say two "foreign" words, "symposium" and "seminar," in the same breath, he blurted out "synanon": "I want to get into another one of those—symp——sem——synanons!" In this way, a new word was introduced into the language to describe a new social phenomenon.

---

[1]Abraham H. Maslow, "Synanon and Eupsychia," *Journal of Humanistic Psychology*, Spring 1967.

Yablonsky writes about Synanon

> Synanon is more than symposiums and seminars. It is *a new kind of group therapy* [author's italics]; an effective approach to racial integration; a humane solution to some facets of bureaucratic organization; a different way of being religious; *a new method of attack therapy* [author's italics]; an unusual kind of communication; and an exciting, fresh approach to the cultural arts and philosophy.[2]

It is interesting to note that Synanon was founded with the advent of the new group therapies. Synanon was founded in 1958, and it was at that time that the first encounter groups began to appear.

Psychotherapy is conceptually composed of a few fundamental principles, which while difficult of application, are easily seized upon by the laity for their specific purposes. In the Synanon groups, for example, hostile confrontation between members is encouraged in what it calls "games," and it offers certainly immediate catharsis of aggressive feelings in a most volatile form. As such, it is directly derived from psychoanalysis! This is not surprising when one realizes that Alcoholics Anonymous provides a twenty-four-hour transferential figure of a specific superego kind while it exhorts the ego to stand up for itself and stop drinking. In a sense, and Synanon is included in it, these are self-help movements and are similarly based upon one or another analytic principle, although most of them will deny this.

Synanon is just another example of a new group

---

[2]Lewis Yablonsky, *Synanon: The Tunnel Back* (Baltimore: Pelican Books, 1965), p. viii.

therapy, which appeared to be helpful for those patients who were not being reached by traditional psychotherapy. It is pretty much well known that traditional psychotherapy is not very well equipped or had not been designed to handle the addictive personality.

Perhaps the most controversial element of the Synanon groups is their profound belief that people can help themselves without standard professional therapy or therapists. This is one of the most important aspects (and also perhaps one of the most dangerous ones) of the new encounter groups, which took so much from the addiction groups. There is a strong trend among the new encounter groups to do without any professional therapists. That such poses serious questions as to the responsibility of the group members needs no answer. Who is able, without being a professional therapist, to diagnose severely disturbed psychotics, and what about the after-care of such cases. Many people in our contemporary society are sitting on explosive bombs, but for some reason or another they are never exploded. However the group experience, such as an encounter group, might just do the trick and who is there to recognize this and moreover to help and understand?

Every professional therapist at this point knows that there has been a significant increase in borderline psychotics and psychotics as such. While Freud might have treated quiet neurotics in the 1920s, we today are faced with a patient who is far more disturbed and potentially violent than in past, even recent, times. To expose such patients to the rather give-and-take, who-cares attitude of the encounter groups and even addiction groups, such as Synanon and Daytop, seems somewhat questionable.

It seems pertinent and fair also to quote Charles Dederich, the founder of Synanon, about the professional position of Synanon:

> We use as much knowledge from as many sources as possible. In Synanon, we quote and use the ideas of Freud, Ralph Waldo Emerson, Lao-tse, and many of the pronouncements of Christ. We use any system of ideas that helps us to better understand the human condition. We use self-training; you know, "going through the motions." We deal with the person's identity in the here and now. We use brainwashing and attack therapy here to peel away those parts of the self that haven't been too effective—in fact, have put the person in the mess he's in. We make him aware of new ideas and ways of behaving. By getting the person to go through certain behavior motions, he is somehow euchred into constructing his own approach to life.[3]

Dederich maintains that in Synanon and its subsequent groups they start "backward from psychoanalysis." While psychonalysis works primarily with the id and the unconscious, they start with behavior and the superego, and then eventually get to the id and the unconscious.

What he means is that in the group interaction there is an emphasis on the conscious rather than on the unconscious motivations of the group members. In such a setting, attack therapy probably works well, where no attempts are made to penetrate the unconscious.

One of the results of Synanon in terms of the

---

[3]*Synanon: The Tunnel Back*, p. 367.

new group therapies, or specifically the encounter groups, is its emphasis on directness or the no-nonsense approach. This too raises questions and Maslow in his essay on Daytop, an offshoot of Synanon, suggests this:

> You see, the problem is the same for psychoanalysis, for individual psychotherapy. The theory that they have developed out of their experience is that it is just this *directness* [author's italics] that will drive people away from therapy. What they do is work people in very gentle and allow them months before they really start digging at the problem. They try to establish a relationship first and then put a little pressure on. This is contradicted here where nobody waits for six months; the intensive therapy starts right away. It is a question of what works best, and for whom, for how many.[4]

Yablonsky who attended about a hundred Synanon sessions first had his doubts about this directness:

> My first reaction to the rugged Synanon was to conclude that the attackers were after "blood" and that somehow this "fixed" their own emotional sadistic needs. I also feared for the victim of the mob. I could see some of the therapeutic rationale for attacking "bad behavior"; but at that time, I felt that the group was "rat-packing" a "victim" and was going too far. However, on the basis of my participation . . . I have revised my early personal opinions about what some professionals have labeled "verbal brutality" . . .

[4]Abraham Maslow, "Synanon and Eupsychia."

> My recognition of the validity of "attack therapy" was gradual. At first, it surprised me tremendously, after a rough session, to see two or more "bitter enemies" come out of the session laughing about their Synanon experience and discussing it in a friendly, jovial manner. After one session I attended, I remember an individual who had been on the "hot seat" (accused of "goofing off" on his job) telling his antagonist later, "You son-of-a-bitch, you really exaggerated my work out of sight—I did most of that work . . . " The former antagonist, now friend, said, "What did you expect? We were in Synanon."[5]

Some questions however are being raised by therapists about the underlying philosophy of the encounter groups, i.e., the human potential movement, and it seems only fair to take some of these questions into account in discussing some of the encounter groups, such as the Synanon groups in this instance.

Albert Ellis, who for a long time has worked with encounter groups, is sharp in his criticism:

> In the long run, the human potential movement is anti-therapeutic . . . Human beings seem to become happier, more creative, more self-directed, less anxious, and less hostile when they change some of their basic irrational and childish assumptions: especially the assumptions (a) that it is a dire necessity for them to be loved or approved by virtually every significant other person they encounter; (b) that they should be thoroughly competent, adequate, and achieving in all

[5]Yablonsky, *op. cit.*, p. 380.

> possible respects if they are to consider themselves worthwhile; (c) that people as a whole, including themselves, are bad, wicked, or villainous when they behave unethically and that they should be severely blamed and punished for their villainy; and (d) that it is awful and catastrophic when things are not the way they should like them to be and when their desires are not immediately gratified. These unrealistic and silly philosophies or value systems are not only uncontradicted by many encounter groups, particularly those of the conventional sensitivity training type, but are actually sustained and enhanced by these groups. Certain Esalen-type and Synanon-oriented marathon groups, for example, wittingly or unwittingly teach their participants that they are worthwhile people if other members of the group will give them a bear hug or that they should *enrage* [author's italics] themselves at other marathon participants who act impolitely or negatively....[6]

Since most professional psychoanalysts are by and large dubious about the encounter groups, they are even more dubious about the Synanon experience. There is a sharp disagreement between the psychoanalytic profession and the Synanon people (and for that matter the encounter group proponents) about what constitute mental health. Most psychoanalysts believe very strongly that a true cure or, if you will, permanent results can only be accomplished by the legitimate profession. Although they

---

[6]Albert Ellis, "A Weekend of Rational Encounter," *Encounter*, Arthur Burton, ed. (San Francisco: Jossey-Bass, 1969). p. 126.

admit that the Synanon groups *provide* the opportunity to reach those who are apparently unreachable by psychoanalysis, they feel that eventually such people will still need psychotherapy after the Synanon experience.

As one psychoanalyst friend of Synanon formulated it, "Synanon is fantastic in bringing the person to the level where he can be reached by psychoanalysis. Because of Synanon we [the professionals] are now in a position to cure the addict."

Still, Dederich has a point when he maintains that the so-called verbal attack therapy fits in the personality patterns of the addict. As he remarked, "Dope fiends shoot dope. As long as they are dope fiends, they are not much good; they are slobs and thieves, with the temperaments of nasty little children. When they stop using dope, they're something else again. They need self-respect and then general respect more than they do sympathy. This will send them running for a fix. Too much laxness with them—particularly in the early stages—makes them take their adjustment problems too lightly. At Synanon, we may seem rough on the newcomer at times, but we have to be their guts, until they develop guts for themselves."

Most important is what came out of Synanon in terms of the new group therapies. There seems little doubt that Synanon has worked as a powerful stimulant in the ongoing process of the encounter groups. That at least Synanon not only reached its own people, however inadequate this might be, but that it also provided the field of group psychotherapy with stimulating new techniques. Abraham Maslow, who participated in some of the Daytop experiences comments:

> May I tell you something. I've been in only one encounter group—last night—and I don't know how I would react if I'd been in that thing for a long time. Nobody has even been that blunt with me in my whole life. It is certainly a striking contrast to the conventional world, the world of university professors. Faculty meetings are certainly not like these encounters. They don't mean a damn thing and I try to avoid them if I can—all the politeness, nobody will say "boo!" If I may say it, I remember thinking of one professor that he would not say "shit" if he were in it up to his neck. Well, this is different; it shook me up a little last night. In the world I come from everyone is so polite because they are avoiding confrontation. There are a lot of prissy old maids around—I mean masculine "old maids." I think it would be a wonderful thing if it were possible for you to get in on one of our faculty meetings and have a real encounter. It would turn the whole thing upside down. And I have a suspicion that it would be for the best.[7]

The breakthroughs achieved in the Synanon groups were of course possible since the group encounter is quite different from the one-to-one relationship. A singular advantage of the group, and the encounter group specifically, is that it automatically makes the medical model of the therapeutic interaction somewhat inappropriate. The terrible disadvantages of such a model are partially modified. Some therapists, for sure, are so engrammed with the model that they can succeed in transposing a group into a

[7]Abraham H. Maslow, "Synanon and Eupsychia."

set of one-to-one medically modeled parallel relationships with the therapist relating technically to a group of diseased patients who are a group only in the sense of their being present at the same time in the same place, related only to God or therapist—depending on their theological tastes. But such of course does not constitute group therapy or even encounter groups. As the group members interact with one another and with the gestalt of the group, the therapist, who is medically and culturally programmed, gets confused, morally disoriented and anxiously inappropriate. Things begin to happen that were never described by William Osler or anticipated by the Hippocratic oath. These happenings are rumbles of encounters. And strange to relate, these happenings have a way of developing their own emergent thrust in groups so that even the therapist who considers personal encountering somewhat sinful finds his disease-oriented philosophy, technical security and compulsive sense of responsibility either disregarded or ignored.

For those of us who have read Yablonsky's book *Synanon: The Tunnel Back* and Endore's more or less fictionalized account, *Synanon,* it is clear that what came out of Synanon in terms of the new encounter groups was its stress on honesty and forthrightness, its direct no-nonsense approach to the person's problems and the pressure brought upon the patient, a pressure he simply could not get away from. But we should also realize that such an approach did not mean a refutation of psychoanalysis, a belief many maintained and still do. Psychoanalysis *never* was intended to work for the kind of disturbed, addictive people who had literally hit rock-bottom when they came to Synanon. It seems timely to state here quite strongly since so many of the people who work in Synanon or even in other encounter groups have not the slightest notion about the kind of psychoanalysis Freud conceived and developed. It is a gross injustice to Freud and his work to state simply that psychoanalysis has failed with addicts or for that matter with other rather disturbed people who flock to the marathons. He never intended that it would. For those who would take the time and read some of Freud's own prerequisites for the work-ability of psychoanalysis to a given individual should read his early paper "On Psychotherapy" (1904):

> One should look beyond the patient's illness and form an estimate of his whole personality; those patients who do not possess a reasonable degree of education and a fairly reliable character should be refused . . . one should limit one's choice of patients to those who possess a *normal mental condition* [author's italics], since in the psychoanalytic method this is used as a foothold from which to obtain control of the morbid manifestations. Psychoses, states of confusion and deeply-rooted (I might say toxic) depression are therefore not suitable for psychoanalysis . . .[8]

It seems unfortunate that many defenders of the Synanon experience have placed the type of work that is being done at Synanon as opposed to psychoanalysis, while it is obvious that Synanon and the new encounter groups are simply a form of therapy, perhaps not even psychotherapy, which has found

[8]Sigmund Freud, "On Psychotherapy" (1904), *Standard Edition,* Vol. VII, pp. 263–64.

new approaches to problems, such as addiction, in our society.

When one reads Endore's *Synanon* one is struck by the preponderance of dialogue and confrontation, not so much with the nonverbal techniques. But as one ponders for a while one realizes that we discovered from Jacques Lacan[9] that psychoanalysis, besides many other things, was "the talking cure," that it was an epistemology of discourse, that it was concerned with the *communication* and *relationship* between *subjects*—rather than simply that between analysts and patients—and that the interpretation of dreams, all in all, meant the interpretation of discourse, for the dream was above all a *translation* and a *message*.

So we might have returned to one of our original theses in this book, that a great deal of what is going on in the new group psychotherapies found its roots in the principles and practice of psychoanalysis and psychotherapy. Traditional psychoanalysis and psychotherapy could not of course foresee the vast changes in the societal structure which in turn produced the people who come to Synanon and the encounter groups. Who could, for example, have expected the enormous increase in drug addiction of the past decades? It is interesting to note that Alethea Hayter in planning a book on the effect of opium addiction on the creative imagination of nineteenth-century writers thought she was investigating a mental phenom-

---

[9]See Jacques Lacan, *The Language of the Self: The Function of Language in Psychoanalysis* (Baltimore: The Johns Hopkins Press, 1968). See also Jacques Lacan, *Ecrits* (Paris: Editions du Seuil, 1966) and Jacques Lacan, "Some Reflections on the Ego," *International Journal of Psychoanalysis*, XXXIV (1953), pp. 11–17.

enon of the past but discovered in 1967 that her book was actually most timely![10]

Perhaps it is even unfair to classify Synanon as a form of group psychotherapy or even a new form of group interaction, because the Synanon people themselves do not see it that way. As Endore remarks:

> But don't confuse it with group therapy. Because it isn't group therapy at all. It's a game. It's a contest. It's a sport. It's a vigorous workout for the mind and the emotions. It will strain your brain and your vocal cords, and for all I know your spleen too. And if it's therapeutic, as it most certainly seems to be, then it's partly for the same reasons that any sport is healthful, because it's strenuous enough to stimulate your bloodstream, raise your pulse rate, excite your senses, stir up your feelings, and leave you afterward refreshed and pleasantly exhausted.[11]

Certainly when we look at the setting of the Synanon groups it becomes clear that this is not group therapy, either straight or even way-out. The sessions are administered by a group of peers who have similar problems. Because of a similarity of life experiences and identifications, a fellow Synanist is more likely to be acceptable as a "therapist." Also apparently in this setting the Synanist is not being seen as an authority figure in the usual sense. Also Synanists reverse roles as "patient" and "therapist" in the group sessions. Synanon maintains that this rever-

---

[10]Alethea Hayter, *Opium and the Romantic Imagination* (London: Faber & Faber, 1968).

[11]Guy Endore, *Synanon* (New York: Doubleday, 1968), p. 169.

sal of roles provides the participant with some insights into his own problems in the process. However, this is not much different even from orthodox group therapy where all participants change roles in terms of patients and therapists. The only difference is that in the orthodox group there is the presence of a professional therapist. The Synanists also maintain that there is a democratic approach to psychological interaction in that there is an absence of the doctor-patient relationship. However I know for sure that in many of the encounter groups (and even in quite a few of the orthodox groups) there is hardly anymore a pronounced relationship of *doctor-patient.* In many encounter groups the therapists are participants and are called by their first name. They often discuss their own personal experiences and even their own feelings about the participants.[12] They do get angry and express themselves freely like the other participants.

Since Synanon is a community where the participants are living together the emotional growth of each member is naturally much more of a going concern for each of them. But that is much more the result of communal living than of a difference in approach to group therapy.

Maslow in his essay raised another interesting point on the Synanon and Daytop experiences.

> You can talk about psychological health, about being mature and strong, adult and creative, mostly as a consequence of this psychological medicine—like vitamins . . . The question is, does Daytop supply these psychological vitamins? My impression as I

[12]See Hendrik M. Ruitenbeek, "A Note on the Participation of the Group Psychotherapist," in *Group Therapy Today.*

> wandered around this place this morning is that it does. Remember what they are: first of all, safety, being anxiety-free, free of fear; next, belongingness, you have to belong to a group; next, affection, you have to have people who like you; and finally, respect, you have to have some respect from people. Could it be that Daytop is effective because it provides an environment where these feelings are possible?

Our question is what happens to these people when they leave the safe surroundings of Daytop and Synanon. Have they received and absorbed enough security and *identity feeling,* sense of self, if you will, that they are able to go on their own? One of the essential theses of all therapy groups is that we try to provide the participants with enough resources and strength so that they are able to face the world *outside* the group. I am sure it is nice and cozy to have it all packaged in some closed-off community but that does not constitute the world *we* live in although this community might very well reflect a great deal of that world. Are the Synanon members perhaps *too* sick to function in the world at large, and does Synanon and Daytop in effect provide them with the opportunity to escape from the world that they could not face in the first place?

The degree of sickness is perhaps more important than we are apt to think, in terms of working with patients in encounter groups. I might suggest that one cannot encounter sickness, nor can you encounter with sickness. The encounter, by definition, is a *healthy* experience, perhaps a health-giving experience. This is true even if the person relating out of his health has considerable sickness in his person. The concept of encounter thus implies a basic assumption in psychotherapy—that of growth. Growth as *change* means the isolation and enhancement of the residual health in a patient, disregarding the sickness relatingly,* although cognitively we may be constantly aware of it as interfering, impassing, and subjectively as nonhealth.

What Synanon brought the encounter experience cannot be underestimated; it stressed the elements of intensity and confrontation and showed that these should be essential to any worthwhile and fruitful group experience. Admittedly it also reached a type of patient who so far had been at loose ends in terms of cure and adjustment. And so it showed us once more that the field of personal interrelations is vast and unlimited in its scope.

A last aspect of the Synanon experiment that should be considered is its link to the concept of the communes. After all people live together, work together, and share together their problems. Fritz Perls in his autobiography *In and Out the Garbage Pail,* feels that the present trend in group therapy is to move away from even the new group meetings and to institute so-called Gestalt kibbutzes. Fritz Perls writes:

> What do I mean by Gestalt kibbutz? As I had previously considered individual therapy to be obsolete, so I now consider the piecemeal group meetings and workshops to be out-of-date. The marathon meetings are too forced. I propose now to conduct the following experiment. In the kibbutz, the split between seminarians and staff has to be

*The emphasis in both individual and group therapy should be on *health* rather than on the sickness and pathology of the patient.

> abolished. All the work has to be done by the people coming to the kibbutz. Permanent staff: 1) the caretaker and developer, someone who has a background in building, etc. 2) the therapist. The main accent is on developing a community spirit and maturation. There will be a turnover every month of ten leaving and ten arriving. There will be organic and vegetable farming and a craft shop for making simple furniture.[13]

Synanon is probably closest to the description and definition of Perls's new therapy kibbutzes. To what degree, we are still doing therapy is another question. After all there have been communes throughout the centuries. The very fact that they are now announced as an offspring of the new politics, the new left and an anti-establishment attitude, perhaps an anticapitalist Maoist movement, does not mean that sociologically they differ much from the early Shaker communes or the various communist-oriented communes of the nineteenth-century, which were fairly prevalent in Europe and America. If one reads Gail Sheehy's account of an interview with a young revolutionary, living in a commune near Columbia University,[14] one only can be struck by the degree of psychopathology that seems to pervade his mind and existence. I doubt that contemporary communes have in a way much in common with the older communes, but which ideologically were stronger based and still ended up in miserable failure.

I do not see a development away from group-oriented therapy to commune-oriented therapy as

---

[13]Frederick S. Perls, *In and Out the Garbage Pail* (Lafayette, Cal.; Real People Press, 1969).

[14]Gail Sheehy, "Bombing on the Mind," *New York*, April 6, 1970.

necessarily a healthy one. It seems to me that the inability of the individual to survive (not cope) in the world is at stake, both in a therapeutic and in a larger political and social sense.

There seems to be a great deal of unreality in the argumentation of those participating in such communes or similar enterprises,* there certainly is little chance that they will change society at large (even if they are interested in that), but on top of that I would venture to say that most of them contain psychological dropouts, whose neurotic frustrations have blocked their creative talents and shattered whatever discipline they had to fulfill even limited goals in their life situation. Now that in itself might not be all that serious, but I do not see why we should consider them as the prophets of the *now.*

We have to be careful that we do not confuse the scope of the new group therapies—and that includes Synanon and Perls's projected therapeutic kibbutzes—and political and social movements. After all, those who participate in the new group therapies come primarily to find themselves, to get hold of themselves and perhaps, if they are lucky, gain some new perspective on their life situations. Those participating in the new social and political movements are there, as we should assume, primarily to do something about a frustrated world situation. That their motivations somehow will get confused is only understandable in such a complex world as ours.

In returning to Synanon it seems appropriate to state here that psychotherapy and group therapy are an ongoing process and they certainly can take to

*I have been told that communes or at least communities resembling them are now fairly frequent in New Mexico and California.

heart the lessons learned at Synanon and Daytop. It has certainly enlarged the scope of group therapy and thus reached some who so far were isolated and desperate.

THE NUDE GROUP THERAPIES

Next to the taboo of touch there is the taboo of nudity in psychotherapy. The question of nude psychotherapy especially has become pertinent in the new group therapies. Since a free spirit has broken through in the various encounter groups the question of taking off one's clothes inevitably had to come up! But why? Is it necessary to take off one's clothes in order to relate? Or for that matter, in order to be intimate?

Paul Bindrim, who probably has written one of the most sensible and sensitive articles about nude group therapy, maintains that

> these spontaneous excursions into nudity seem to increase interpersonal transparency,

> remove inhibitions in the area of physical contact, decrease the sense of personal isolation and estrangement, and culminate in a feeling of freedom and belongingness.[1]

Alexander Lowen, who certainly has pioneered in the psychotherapy of touch and nudity in his various bioenergetic theories, feels that

> nakedness is the great leveler of social distinctions for it reduces all persons to the common bodily or animal level on which they came into the world. Nudity strips the individual of his ego pretensions and, sometimes, of his ego defenses . . . Nudity removes all privacy and reduces all pride.[2]

I certainly cannot be that enthusiastic about the removal of privacy, or for that matter the reduction of pride. Both still play an important role in the social interaction between human beings in our society.

The naked body tends to state and emphasize the sexual aspects of one's personality. Because of our standards of morality and modesty there is in the mind of many an identification between the nude body and sexuality. We cover the genital area and thus cover in a sense our sexuality. There are contrary opinions however on this point. J. C. Flugel in his well-known book, *The Psychology of Clothes* felt that "nakedness tends to diminish sexuality," and he thought that when erotic feelings were transferred to the total body, the focus upon the genitals dimin-

---

[1]Paul Bindrim, "A Report on a Nude Marathon," *Psychotherapy* (Fall 1968), Vol. 5, No. 3.

[2]Alexander Lowen, "In Defense of Modesty," *The Journal of Sex Research*, (February 1968), Vol. 4, No. 1, pp. 52, 53.

ishes. It also seems the experience of many nudist organizations that the increased pleasure of exhibitionism and of skin and muscle eroticism drained off a certain quantity of sexual energy that might otherwise have found a purely genital channel.

The raison d'être for nudity in psychotherapy, both group and individual, seems to be that the inviolable sense of privacy that man maintains by wrapping himself in a tower of clothes or retreating to the castle of his home might not only safeguard his individuality, but also perhaps, in effect, be a self-imposed padded cell through which he can limit his contact when he basically distrusts and fears interaction with other persons.[3]

Those who are in favor of the nude encounter groups feel strongly that the disrobing might constitute a symbolic attempt to open, so to say, a cell of isolated psychological privacy to healthy group interaction and intimacy. Abraham Maslow also raised the question of the nude encounter:

> After all, these training groups are a kind of psychological nudism under careful direction. I wonder, as a matter of fact, what would happen as an experiment, if these T-groups remained exactly as they are but only added a physical nudism. People would go away from there an awful lot freer, a lot more spontaneous, less guarded, less defensive; not only about the shape of their behinds, or whether their bellies are hanging or not, but freer and more innocent about their minds, as well. If I can learn not to be conscious about the fact that my ass is hanging or that my belly sticks out too much,

[3]See Paul Bindrim, *op. cit.*

> if I can throw off this fear, this defense, maybe this act of freedom will enable me thereby to throw off a lot of other defenses—maybe the defense of looking ignorant, or uncontrolled, or something like that.[4]

The reader would of course also be interested in knowing more about the composition, location and living arrangements of a nude marathon. Bindrim, in his article, details the arrangements:

> Announcements of the proposed nude marathon were sent out to psychologists, marriage counselors, participants in group and individual therapy, and persons who had attended previous marathons. Dr. William E. Hartman, professor of sociology at California State College, acted as co-therapist* with the author. Dr. Hartman was assisted by Marilyn Fithian, A. B., a college instructor of folklore and marriage classes. The author was assisted by Sara McClure, B. S., a dance therapist. Twenty participants registered for the marathon and were initially screened by telephone interviews. A small reduction in fee was extended to married and unmarried couples, in an attempt to keep an even balance of sexes. This was felt to be important, since it was anticipated that the initial effect of nudity would be expressed in terms of sexual curiosity, which made it desirable that there be an equal number of

---

[4]Abraham Maslow, *Eupsychian Management: A Journal* (Homewood, Ill.: R. D. Irwin, 1965), p. 160.

*The idea of the co-therapist is fairly popular with marathon leaders. It relieves them of some of the strain and adds the creativity of another therapist to the marathon. (Ruitenbeek)

men and women in attendance. Since more males than females registered, a few single women were offered reduced rates as an inducement for them to attend the marathon, thus maintaining the balance of the sexes, namely ten males and ten females. Minors were not admitted. The occupations of the persons attending included three engineers, two school teachers, four clinical psychologists, a pharmacist, two magazine editors, two social workers, an artist, and a number of housewives. Two of the participants were referred by clinical psychologists who felt that their symptoms would be helped by the experience of social nudity. A few of the participants had prior experience with social nudity at nudist camps, but the majority either had had no prior experience, or their previous experiences had been limited to one or two occasions when they experienced nudity with a small group of their own selection. Two of the participants were a married couple; others were married but came without their mates; and the majority were single.

The location was Deer Park Nudist Camp near Escondido, California. Deer Park occupies an entire valley between two mountain ranges, is approximately four hundred acres in size, affords privacy, a beautiful natural setting, with abundant fruit trees and wildlife, and is equipped in a comparable fashion to a high-class resort hotel. It had just closed its operations to the general public so that the marathon group had complete privacy on the grounds. Its facilities included a large swimming pool, surrounded by cabanas, and a Jacuzzi bath, which was kept at a temperature of 102 degrees, and was large enough to accommodate the entire group. The group

> brought sleeping bags and air mattresses and slept in the open around the pool and in the surrounding cabanas. Meetings were held indoors and outdoors, depending on the weather. Climate conditions were at times unfavorable, occasionally requiring the wearing of clothing for comfort. Meals were served cafeteria style while the group remained in session.[5]

From the available literature it becomes clear that a high premium is being placed in the nude encounter groups on the sensory experience. In one of Bindrim's groups it was suggested that the participants bring with them things that they enjoyed smelling the most, touching the most, tasting the most, and hearing the most for the specific purpose as stimuli in a sensory saturation experience, which would induce some kind of a peak experience, almost like a mild "turn-on."

Bindrim describes this kind of an experience in the following words:

> The Sunday morning session included one hour which was devoted to meditation, facilitated by sensory saturation with peak stimuli. In this procedure, the participants chose partners of the opposite sex by gazing into each other's eyes for a few moments and then selecting the person with whom eye contact was the most comfortable and relaxing. They were then seated close to and facing the person of their choice. They were then asked to close their eyes and to keep them closed until asked to open them, following which they were given suggestions conducive to relaxation. Each participant was asked to simultaneously taste, touch, and

[5]Paul Bindrim "*A Report On A Nude Marathon.*"

smell the items which he enjoyed the most and had selected for the experiment. For example, one participant simultaneously touched velvet, ate chocolate, and smelled a rose. These items were, of course, different for each participant. During this period the prelude to Tristan and Isolde, by Wagner, was played on a record player. This process of sensory saturation led to a mild drugless "turn-on" or peak state of experiencing. In this state, the participants were asked to re-experience in fantasy whatever event in their lives they considered to be the best moment that they had ever lived; a time when they flowed freely in the joy of living and felt close to the core of their being and at one with life. When they each had completed this fantasy recall of a peak experience and were "turned-on" within the limits of their capabilities, they were asked to touch the fingertips of both hands with their partners and to quietly gaze into each other's eyes without movement or distraction, allowing themselves to open to each other and experience a growing sense of intimacy and at-one-ment. During this time, the Love Death from Tristan and Isolde was played. After twenty minutes of this eye-centered meditation, they were asked to place their chairs in a circle and share their experiences.[6]

As in some of the other encounter groups there seems to be an emphasis here on the nonverbal techniques, and one has to admit that probably totally new areas of human experience are opened up for those who are essentially locked in their own selves.

What are the reactions of some participants to

[6]Paul Bindrim, *op. cit.*

the introduction of nudity in the encounter group? Here follows some of the reactions of some members of a nude marathon:

> *Ken*: "This is entirely new to me. I've never had any occasion with a group of people to be nude, and I'm scared to death. I think that Lou said it better than I could say it—that I was not so much inhibited as I'm scared of my reaction to other people, and of course scared to death of having an erection."
>
> *Greg*: "I've never tried it before, and I'll say that I have some inhibitions about it, mild to moderate."
>
> *Lee*: "I feel quite sensitive, both from the standpoint of being looked at and more so from the standpoint of looking at other people. I don't know exactly why I should, but that's what I want to find out."
>
> *Ted*: "As I mentioned to Vicky earlier, I wasn't going to be the first, but I wasn't going to be the last one either."
>
> *Joan*: "This is my first experience in anything like this, including therapy, but I feel kind of included in the group; I'm not sure though if one weekend is quite enough."[7]

One of the main questions is in terms of the nude marathon: What about the place of sexuality in all of this? Although there are rules about not showing sexual signals, so to say, a nude marathon obviously poses questions in this area. Bindrim maintains that as a marathon proceeds the tendencies to look excessively or to experience self-consciousness when being looked at *diminished* to a point where many of the partici-

[7]Paul Bindrim, *op. cit.*

pants would have probably been unable to report whether others were or were not wearing clothing.

He noticed that full body contact became more and more spontaneous and less sexually oriented. He also felt that overt sexual expression was undoubtedly inhibited by the presence of the group and the ground rules, which were set forth at the beginning of the marathon. What then are some of the aspects of the *nude* marathon, which might be different from a regular marathon?

Participants maintain first of all that they derive a sense of pleasure from the freedom to look at other persons' bodies and from the feeling to be looked at themselves.

They apparently experience a personal sense of *comfort*, exhilaration and freedom. As one of the participants in a nude marathon remarked: "I felt very much more comfortable being undressed than dressed. When dressed, I feel I have to sit up straight, keep my back up and all that. Undressed, I feel it's all open and so I feel very good, being undressed." They also experience pleasure from the sense of group closeness, which is expressed in the relaxed expressions on the faces of the participants. "I'd like to tell Jack what a marvelous look of pleasurable wonderment I saw cross his face when he hit the water* in the pool last night. I haven't seen an expression like that except on a child's face when something marvelous happened and everything's all right." Too, the participants experience a sense of naturalness of the nude condition and a feeling of relief at not having reacted inappropriately. "And

*Most nude marathons take place in facilities where heated swimming pools are available.

speaking of erections, I looked at a girl, especially your body, Anita, and I could catch myself concentrating on it and I could feel a tickling in my genitals and I found that if I concentrated, if all my thoughts were on this, then I could have an erection very easily, but if it is *diffused* [author's italics], it's just like going about everyday life, and I found it quite pleasurable." Some of the participants experienced being high or unable to sleep for most of the remainder of the night following the first day of the nude marathon. "I laid awake the entire night. The stimuli that had been created by the nudity, I think, allowed a great deal of thought in my mind all night." One question might be raised here. Does the *diffusion* really work? Is there perhaps a sense of frustration in lying awake the whole night because of the sexual stimuli received during the day? Would it not have been better to verbalize this nonverbal reaction?

Some of the participants in the nude marathon also experienced a sense of concern about one's physical body when comparing it with other members of the group. ". . . and the other reaction that I was aware of was feeling that my genitals perhaps weren't as large as the other men's, and this was a matter of some concern, although I didn't think about it much, but as I sit here now I know I was concerned." Another participant: "The funny thing is that I have the same kind of negative feelings about my body." The last statement might force us to pause and wonder if the exposure in the nude in encounter groups are really all that valuable? Let us look for a moment at the follow-up session of this marathon and notice some of the reactions of the participants.

"For a period of several months I've been in a kind of metamorphosis. I guess I can call it for lack of a better word, an emerging. If we can think about my emerging like this [gestures, indicating slow uphill plane] our time together kind of this [indicates rapid upswing], a kind of zoom . . ."

"Ted felt the marathon was beneficial in some ways. He said he's been in therapy for seven or eight years and he's never been able to work through his relationships with his father before, and he thought that was the most significant thing that happened at the marathon."

"Since the marathon I find myself smiling every once in a while, and I think the reason is the memory I have of how I so easily related to the men, without any fear of being rejected."

Those who participated in nude marathons do maintain that nudity apparently facilitated group interaction in a given marathon. In the marathon conducted by Paul Bindrim seventeen of the twenty participants felt that the factor of nudity increased their ability to open up to each other emotionally and to achieve a greater degree of authenticity and transparency. Bindrim felt that this group became therapeutically functional more rapidly than in the clothed marathon groups.

Participants in a nude marathon do feel that nudity in a group that encourages skin contact seems to be therapeutic in itself. This is perhaps needed to compensate for the sensory isolation experienced by the individual in his normal clothed state.* It may be assumed that our social world outside of the home is frequently experienced as a jungle of polite estrangement where physical and emotional contact is prohibited by walls, locked doors, clothing, status roles, and a variety of other masks. Bindrim maintains that

*Is sensory isolation not a part of a general isolation experienced by the individual in a technological society?

"nudity in itself may represent a symbolic and factual lifting of the mask which constitutes an invitation to tribal unity and which is most effective when a reversion to the established pattern of private paired relationships is inhibited by blocking sexual expression and subgrouping."

Lowen, et al., have proved beyond a shade of a doubt that the relationship between body image and emotional problems is obvious, and let us not forget that self-acceptance, in many cases, is associated with body image. So it might be possible that in this respect, much can be accomplished by the open discussion of what the individual feels are his undesirable physical characteristics. We all know that these are frequently distortions in his own thinking which might be best remedied by open exposure to group reaction, thus increasing his ego strength and mobilizing his deeper emotional conflicts.

The prevalence of sexuality in the nude marathon is not too surprising when one considers the stress that is being placed on sexuality in our contemporary society. There is a standing rule in the nude marathons on the exposure of overt sexual expressions. This inhibition of overt sexual expression during the marathon is probably beneficial to individuals who would employ sexual activity as a defense against emotional closeness. For many sexually inhibited participants it might be even unfortunate that our present social mores prevent a more generous sexual attitude in the therapeutic group.

In the discussion of the nude encounter group it seems also pertinent to state that in our society sensual body contact is generally considered to be an invitation to sexual intimacy. The inhibition of sexual intimacy by our mores thus also inhibits body contact. And we know that since body contact is frequently essential to emotional expression, this taboo of touch blocks a vital avenue of communication.

Such is of course most obvious in the relationships between males in this country. They are inhibited in expressing any kind of physical affection, or even expression of their love, since any embrace or experience of body contact might carry the implication of homosexuality. Where in European countries, especially in France and Italy, such body contact between males (and heterosexual males at that) is quite frequent; it still is a taboo in this society. A nude marathon might eliminate the confusion between tender body contact and overt homosexuality by encouraging sensuality while in a sense inhibiting sexuality and in effect increasing the range of *permissible* emotional expression for both sexes.

In his previously cited paper Bindrim feels that the nude marathon in general requires two steps. A permissive group setting in which participants express their reactions to intimacy that they inhibit in society and in clothed marathons. And he cites the example of voyeuristic and exhibitionistic tendencies, the need to touch and to be touched and the anxieties that are relative to body image and sexual potency. Bindrim feels very strongly that *once* these factors which limit intimacy and authenticity are openly expressed and mobilized in their most basic forms, they are open to the therapeutic intervention of the therapist and the group.

In another article which appeared elsewhere Bindrim touches on the subject of the kind of leader that should conduct the nude marathon. And he states quite appropriately:

> . . . sensitivity training has been criticized—and rightly—for the use of untrained and un-

> supervised leaders, offer neither screening applicants nor providing follow-up, and for not testing its theories. None of these objections applies to the marathons I conduct. Half of the participants already have been prescreened in a sense, for they have been referred by other psychologists and psychiatrists. In addition, each participant is screened preliminarily by telephone and must agree to regard the first part of the marathon itself as a screening process, with the understanding that if I ask him to leave, he will go immediately. While this is not ideal, it serves as a compromise between the excessive costs of pretesting and the blind commitment to work with just anyone who shows up for a marathon.[8]

Such safeguards are the least a marathon therapist can ask for. The field is already overcrowded* by those who have had not adequate therapeutic training either in individual therapy or group therapy.

Although the literature on the nude encounter groups is still small some of the nude group therapists already have noticed certain gains in the treatment of frigid females, impotent males and sexual exhibitionists, where at least they have become temporarily symptom-free. I especially stress the term symptom-free since it implies that the underlying pathological processes have not been touched, and I maintain that such is probably in general the case. That does not in the least diminish the case for the nude encounter groups or for encounter groups in general, but it

---

[8]Paul Bindrim, "Nudity as a Quick Grab for Intimacy in Group Therapy," *Psychology Today* (June 1969), Vol. 3, No. 1.

*In my last chapter I will touch in more detail upon the increase in untrained group therapists.

states an important point in terms of long-range expectations of the patient involved. I am more doubtful about some of the other results that Bindrim cites in his article just quoted.

> Long-standing bachelors who could not commit themselves emotionally have married. Depressed individuals have been freed of suicidal tendencies. Psychotics in remissions have lost their compulsive gestures and behaved normally by the end of the session.[9]

This all sounds very fine. But what about a follow-up of the marriages of such bachelors who married after *one* nude marathon session? Bachelors do not stay single without a reason and these reasons might be very well justified and right. What is the influence of group pressure there? And we certainly are aware that psychotics have their spontaneous remissions, so nude marathons certainly do not necessarily prove such a point. In effect one may ask, what does *one* nude marathon prove here?

If anything, I feel that the importance of nude marathons is to be found in the discovery of the body by the participants. We apparently live in an uptight society (as we are told daily), and one of the characteristics of uptight people is that they are unable to feel, and in this society especially, to touch other people. The fact that the nude marathon provides the opportunity for the rigid patient to experience touching and, as a result, more feeling being produced, should be noted as a positive outcome of such marathons. I am also sure that there are many people

---

[9]Paul Bindrim, *op. cit.*

in our society who do not have to take their clothes off in order to reach their feelings and emotions. For those among us who suffer most from the restrictions of a repressive morality the discovery of one's nudity and the joy of experiencing physical touch through participation in a nude marathon (or any marathon, for that matter) can only be cited as one of the positive aspects of such marathons.

THE THEME GROUPS

In the rush of the new group therapies little attention has been paid to those new group therapies, which perhaps are not as spectacular or intriguing as encounter groups, but which nevertheless have departed from the orthodox group therapy and have come up with new and refreshing procedures.

Theme-centered group psychotherapy has not received the kind of almost sensational attention that other new forms of group psychotherapy have, perhaps because theme-centered group psychotherapy considers itself very much a part of group therapy and does not reject the principles of psychoanalysis, which so many of the encounter therapies have done.

One of the most outstanding exponents of the

theme-centered group psychotherapy is Ruth Cohn, a New York psychoanalyst, who has trained many young group therapists in the workshops she has been conducting for quite a few years.

Her interest in theme-centered workshops started when she initiated a workshop in countertransference, which was designed for the study and treatment of countertransference through self-analysis, in a workshop setting. She discovered that self-analysis, when communicated in the group, initiated a dynamic network of case-related transferences as well as a continuing group process.

Thus she found that the therapist who revealed* himself and his relationship with the patient to the group in free associations stimulated interactional responses in his listeners.[1] In the following case Ruth Cohn describes her own and the group's reactions to her approach to one of her patients:

> Irene was a schizoid woman of 52. I had the feeling that something in my attitude toward her was strange. I had, however, never given it much thought, since I had felt comfortable with the patient and her therapeutic progress, I wondered, while I talked about Irene to the group, why I had chosen this specific case as a countertransference problem. I had treated the patient very cautiously, I remembered thinking that

---

*It might sound strange but many therapists are still very reluctant to participate in any kind of a group where they have to reveal themselves, even if the participants, as in Ruth Cohn's workshop, were only therapists.

[1]Ruth Cohn, "From Couch to Circle to Community: Beginnings of the Theme-Centered Interactional Method" in Hendrik M. Ruitenbeek, ed., *Group Therapy Today.*

she might have a psychotic episode if I applied pressure. When I talked to the group I felt insecure. It occurred to me that I really could not seriously believe Irene would ever break down. She had lived through severe difficulties and crises all her life without psychotic episodes. Had I rationalized my over-cautious handling of the patient for some reason? Irene was a chemist of world fame. I admired her precise mind. She seemed as efficient in analyzing herself in my presence as she was in analyzing chemical ingredients. Any comment or interpretation on my part seemed to fall flat or was refuted by the patient immediately. I felt comfortable in my sessions with her, trustfully leaving the lead to the patient. Irene associated, commented, interpreted, asked questions. I followed her initiative. She was lively, brilliant, interesting. The more I talked to the group about Irene, the more I felt discomfort with my strangely dependent and complacent behavior toward the patient and my (now-obvious) rationalizations. Irene came from a wealthy and cultured, aristocratic background. She lived through an early life of etiquette, sexual and social taboos, and lack of parental warmth. Later on she was cold, successful as a scientist, but in steady combat with her colleagues and frigid as a woman. I decided to use free associations around the topic of "Irene" (as one might use free associations around a dream). Thoughts about Irene's life, her mannerisms, her behavior with me, my feelings during sessions with her, memories she had evoked in me, feelings I shared with her or could not empathize with, all this went through my mind and was immediately communicated to the group, together with seemingly unrelated images, feelings, and thoughts. Slowly, while I associated in this way, the listening group entered into my awareness. I looked at my colleagues' faces and felt an urge to hear from them, to be understood, to be responded to. I "drank in" their expressions. Finally, awareness of the group flooded out all other thoughts. I asked the group urgently to respond to my quest, to tell me what happened to me with this patient. I felt that the group had all the answers, that I had to listen to what they would say, that *they knew*. The group members responded with their own personal associations with increasing speed, ease, and lack of restraint. There were questions, suggestions, and interpretations. Despite my feeling that *they knew*, my mind weighed speedily and carefully all that was brought to me. I responded by accepting or rejecting what was said until the ever-increasing speed and tension broke in the sudden lighting of an emotional recognition: I had experienced Irene as I had experienced my father when I was a child: superior, remote, knowing. All I could do when I was with Irene was to listen with humility, as I used to sit on a little Mexican stool near my father, listening to him with a feeling of quiet contentment that he knew it all, but also with a gnawing feeling of despair about his remoteness to me while he seemed to be close to the people he talked about, adult people and their concerns. I felt the group's release of tension together with my own. For days afterwards, the experience stayed with me. I saw the faces of my young colleagues, intently listening and eager to help. I heard their associa-

> tions, comments, interpretations, re-experienced the growing volume in speed, my momentary blankness and helplessness in looking at the group, the climactic release. Overwhelmingly in the foreground of this repeated postexperience of the session was a feeling of gratefulness to the group: eight people had given me their ability to understand and wish to help; eight people had understood and helped me. The countertransference disturbance with my patient had vanished. I could work with the patient systematically without withdrawing into meaningless passivity.[2]

Out of the countertransference workshop grew other workshops with a single theme and gradually Ruth Cohn developed the theme-groups in terms of the larger community, including the business community. She initiated such workshops as "Encounter and Interpretation," "Freedom and Control in the Psychotherapeutic Relationship," "Body Awareness and Body Touch in Psychotherapy," and other such seminars. Many lay people found her workshops on the following themes very helpful, "Freeing Creativity," "Training Intuition," "Challenge of Change." One of her first consciously selected theme-workshops was "Training in Emotional Skill," and she relates how this weekend seminar (workshop)* met on the weekend President Kennedy was murdered and how Ruth Cohn included the present emotional turmoil into the structure of the weekend workshop. She

[2]Ruth Cohn, "A Group-Therapeutic Workshop on Countertransference," *The International Journal of Group Psychotherapy* (July 1961), Vol. XI, No. 3, p. 284.

*Many of these workshops meet only for a limited time and are not continuous groups.

relates what an intense impact these sessions had, there were tears, empathy, love and scorn. Patients and their anticipated reaction came into focus. They discussed various ways to deal with one's emotions while on the job and how one can use emotions by fusing them in intrapsychic experience with those of the patient ("like letting *my* sadness discover *his*").

The theme-centered workshops have innovated new techniques in the group psychotherapeutic process, which are most helpful for the new group patient. Among the new techniques which Ruth Cohn developed are for example, *silence and thoughts.* Admittedly she feels that these elements have been neglected in psychoanalysis and she writes:

> Although for many years I had occasionally asked patients to be silent rather than to communicate defensively, I had not appreciated the need for silence in psychotherapy as a *necessary element.* We had this weekend experienced silence as a relief (the weekend that President Kennedy had been killed), and a step toward balance. Silence in the group means the experience of being a self *without being alone.* Individuation within a community is an active experience. We live in the many dualities that Nature provides—ebb and tide—; seeding and fruition; separateness and union. We do need both *silence* and communication.[3]

Other techniques, when silence was instructed in the workshop, included: concentrate on thoughts about the given theme, concentrate on feelings and

---

[3]Ruth Cohn, "From Couch to Circle to Community: Beginnings of the Theme-Centered Interactional Method."

experiences of being silently in the group, and concentrate on some special task instructions worked out for the theme under discussion.

Some specific examples include, "Choose one of the people in this group and fantasize in silence something that you might say to him which would be of importance to him." When the silence ends many communications, according to Ruth Cohn, have usually proved to be intuitive, i.e., meaningful to the receiver of the message.

She also relates that in a theme-centered workshop for therapists her request for concentrating upon special task instructions evoked anger about "my lack of responsibility" in not lecturing the workshop about the specific theme, i.e., "Responsiveness and Responsibility of the Psychotherapist," but it also drew reactions of happy acceptance of the challenge to think and feel rather than to have to listen.

There is undoubtedly a great deal of direction on the part of the therapist in the theme-directed groups, but as Ruth Cohn remarked, "Freud advised us to lead the patient to the past if he stays too long in the present and into the present if he ponders about the past." She feels that there is a similarity here in that the theme-centered groups are guiding back and forth between intellectual considerations and emotional experiences, between intrapsychic and interpersonal involvements, between intragroup and outside world phenomena, between strict adherence to the theme and free associations and interactions.

In the larger community the idea of theme-centered group therapy and workshops is extremely helpful, since so many single themes in terms of societal problems can be detected. Ruth Cohn gives a very good example in citing the following case:

In the spring of 1966, influenced by observing an interracial group of therapists who met to explore their own remnant prejudices, I initiated several interracial thematic workshops as a tryout for further interracial work in the community. Winsted Adams, a Negro therapist, and I led a weekend workshop with civil rights workers which was encouragingly successful. We explored relatedness and prejudice within our own group and pursued the cultural experiences which had brought about such feelings within us. We *experienced* (rather than *talked* about*) our distrust and our blocks in communication, and worked at our assorted feelings and thoughts. One white and one Negro woman came to mutually understand their basic dynamics as the result of having been children of isolation who "distrusted everything but cats and trees." A militant Negro teacher became aware of the relevance and usefulness of awareness of personal feelings and internal change in this world. A white teacher rediscovered the need for tender communication which he had forsaken after he grew up. A Negro man was surprised that a white woman liked his looks but disliked his arrogant, boring speeches; he had assumed that the reverse was true. A white man came to understand how his careless forgetting of a phone call has aroused suspicions of prejudice in a Negro worker. At the start of the weekend, the group nearly exploded through the intensity of their hidden hostilities and distrust. At the last session, the group de-

*Note how Ruth Cohn in 1966, before the advent of the encounter groups, already introduced the stress upon *feeling* rather than *talking*.

cided to continue their sessions *without* the departing counselor-leaders.

As a result of Ruth Cohn's theme-centered approach to group psychotherapy many varieties on this theme started appearing in the late sixties. One application, the theme-centered time-limited group has been developed by various group therapists. One of them, Frances Buchanan, related how she became interested in such groups:

> Ten-session groups are a result of being bored. I was bored with open-ended groups as a participant; I was bored with open-ended groups as a therapist. The rambling on and on, seemingly talking, talking, talking about the same things and getting not much of anywhere. The avalanche of words: X was always angry: If X wasn't overtly angry, X was covertly angry—in words. Y whined his way through session after session about being homosexual. Nothing much happened one way or another about it: neither really accepting nor really wishing to change—all in words. Z was fat at the start and for all I know Z is still fat. Nailed to the words.[4]

She also discovered that in the open-ended groups the cutoff point occurred after about ten sessions and only after people settled under "the therapeutic umbrella." So why not a ten-session group and see how that would work? The idea of a single theme hit her at the same time:

---

[4]Frances S. Buchanan, "Notes on Theme-Centered Time-Limited Group Therapy," in *Group Therapy Today.*

> The idea of a theme for a patient group came about when I realized that within my own patient population I had seven attractive, intelligent, hard-working, but isolated people. They related well to me, spoke civilly to their bosses, and maintained a sort of smiling lip-service behavior with others around them, but without involvement or feeling about anyone outside. They maintained their isolation. Faced with seven people who had the same problem, which I felt was not going to be resolved in a talking one-to-one relationship, I simply put them all together, confronting them with the theme of "isolation" and the ten-session correlate. One member of the group later described his life as having been "a comparative course in the dynamics of compulsive futility." He felt that the emotional encounters with the group members had forced him to realize that there are other ways to live. The ten-session limit had also made him aware that if he didn't get into the action, death would find him an isolated, lonely man.[5]

In her theme-centered time-limited groups Frances Buchanan uses other devices, such as the playing of music, the reciting of poetry in order that the participants will use their sensory equipment, their intuition and their perceptiveness of others. She also feels, which is interesting in terms of other encounter groups, that games do not work well since so many people by now have become games-conscious.

Essentially the time-limited group imposes a deprivation upon its members, there is no time for

---

[5]Frances S. Buchanan, *op. cit.*

sitting back and waiting. The participants are forced to act and they set themselves tasks in order to meet the demand of the group, i.e., that its members will actively engage themselves in encounters *outside* the group, the world!

It should be stressed that such time-limited theme-centered groups are by no means a replacement for individual therapy. After all, the resolve of a single problem in a patient's life does not necessarily resolve all of the underlying causes for the patient and he probably will have to tackle those in a more intensive individual therapy.

Much of the effectiveness of such groups, as described by Frances Buchanan, depends entirely on the type of patient who presents himself for treatment, and on the type of psychoanalyst who is conducting this type of group.* We also should realize that we perhaps have arrived at a situation where prospective patients are simply more interested in relieving the symptom than discovering and attacking the underlying cause.

It certainly raises the question of what permanent changes occur in the patient engaged in such group work. It seems appropriate to quote Hans H. Strupp, et al.,[6] who studied reactions of patients to their psychotherapy: "Patients change, but no one is 'cured' in the sense of being restored to a *status quo ante,* nor does there seem to be such a thing as 'spontaneous remission.' . . ." Even Buchanan raises the question of "What are they getting out of this group?" and in a larger sense questions the efficacy of this process. But perhaps since much different

*I will discuss in more detail the role of the new group therapist in the last chapter.

[6]Hans H. Strupp, et. al., *Patients View Their Psychotherapy* (Baltimore: The John Hopkins Press, 1969), p. 141.

techniques are being used we cannot always apply the conventional standards of psychoanalysis. There is a stress in these groups, as in other encounter groups:

> On one occasion, a trouble-maker was a would-be cure guy; the group stopped him by *imposing** silence on him, forbidding him to speak. Since it was an "action" group, they asked him to act, not talk. He refused, standing for most of the session in silent fury. I felt that possibly we had accomplished nothing by this, only supporting his stubbornness to the point where he might not return. The man's response was just the opposite: "It was about time the world told me to shut up. I was angry as hell, but for the first time in my life I *felt* angry!"[7]

In our contemporary society problems and *single* themes are numerous, and we now can have groups on alienation, loneliness, homosexuality,* identity, spontaneity, race, life-goals, etc.

The presentation of a single theme is quite attractive for our contemporary patients. They do live in a fragmented society and it often seems difficult for them to place *all* of their problems in a personal and societal context. The attack by a group on a single problem might at least provide the patient with some focus and perhaps offer him a small perspective in his own confused life.

The single theme does not only apply to the

---

*The directness of this process is illustrated by the word *imposing*, which implies activity.

[7]Frances S. Buchanan, *op. cit.*

*The author once conducted a group of male homosexuals, but must admit that in this case the single theme, i.e., homosexuality was rather limiting and did not produce significant growth results.

particular kind of problem the group might deal with but also to the type of people who participate in the group. My friend Bradford Wilson has conducted for some time a Creative Persons' group,[8] which is not a time-limited group but an *on-going* group, where all participants are artists and where the central theme is their own creativity. In the group it became clear that creativity is not simply a matter of writing, singing, painting, sculpture, etc., but that creativity is rather a *relation* to things which calls upon the individual to do what is needed for himself in his own life at any given moment, to the best of his ability.

Again the spectacular attractiveness of the much talked about encounter groups and marathons might not always be present in the more conventional theme-centered groups, but since most of them, except for the time-limited groups, are *on-going* groups there seems to be more room for long term personal growth. Quick confrontation might relieve the patient momentarily but does not always provide him with the stuff to carry on in his life situation.

---

[8]Bradford Wilson, "The Creative Persons' Group," in *Group Therapy Today.*

THE NEW PATIENT IN GROUP THERAPY

We have traveled a long way from Freud's patients who appeared at Berggasse 19 in Vienna for their analysis with the professor. The type of patient has changed, but not the patient himself. True, every patient is a child of his time and what we have learned, and I am sure of which Freud was very much aware, and that the social context of a given patient also indicates the pattern of his behavior and disturbance. Erik Erikson emphasizes the link between patient and history, so to say, and writes, "... from Freud's patient Dora on, the case histories of neurotically aggravated young people have also demonstrated a relationship *between the epidemiology of a given time and the hidden conflicts of the generations—and thus to history itself* [author's italics][1]." Although Erikson writes here about the young we certainly can apply this to the general relationship of patient and society, patient and history, patient and culture, patient and civilization, and so on.

For example, we hardly see anymore the conversion hysterics in our offices, but the anxiety that our patients communicate to us is, I am sure, the same as Freud experienced in the Berggasse.

Most of his patients were of course from the comfortable upper class in Vienna, they had not been exposed, as our patients, to the traumatic, societal experiences and pressures of our technological society. They could easily identify themselves *and* others, they felt secure and safe in their surroundings, which did not change overnight or even from one generation to another. They grew up in houses and furnishings which did not change every ten years. Many things, which our patients today cannot take for granted, they could and did. The description of Bruno Bettelheim's Chicago school is indicative of the type of household Freud's patients grew up in, "... the school is a Viennese young man's idea of heaven—bourgeois furnishings, a love of art, servants, orderliness, a house full of toys, a strong father image and all you want to eat."[2] I might add to this image a love of music and books, which were always around in great quantities. It is the environment where people sipped tea in their comfortable salons with lots of silver and thick oriental carpets.

There was no talk about a fragmented society

---

[1]Erik H. Erikson, "Reflections on the Dissent of Contemporary Youth," *Daedalus* (Winter 1970), p. 156.

[2]David Dempsey, "Bruno Bettelheim is Dr. No," *The New York Times Magazine* (January 11, 1970), p. 109.

nor about one's identity crisis, alienation or loneliness. Still there were the hidden conflicts within a given generation, as Freud's case of Dora proves, but somehow it was worked out within the given social and personal order and one's life-style and life history. One gets the flavor of the notion of psychoanalytic treatment in those days when one reads what Lou Andreas-Salome* has to say about analytic treatment:

> Tausk† says . . . that analytic treatment alienates the persons involved in it, while most people stress the risk of sexual countertransference. He says also that our piecemeal method of investigation does not lead to an overall picture of the individual. There are of course two basic reasons for this: for one thing, surgical incisions of a face do not improve its beauty, and furthermore, individualized modes of expression yield to a generalized type when the underlying strata are exposed. We have a single common unconscious just as we have a single anatomical structure . . . But I think there is a third factor inherent in the use of the method itself. There is an unalterable contradiction in the application of a method derived from science—the logical analysis by which we gain control of the outer world—to the immediate data of our inmost experiences. It is not simply a question of inspecting psychic

*Lou Andreas-Salome was one of Freud's most beloved pupils. She recorded in her journal *In der Schule bei Freud* (the Freud Journal) her experiences in participating in Freud's Wednesday evening meetings in Vienna.

†Tausk was one of the brighter stars at the analytic horizon in the 1910s. Unfortunately he and Freud came to a separation. See Paul Roazen, *Brother Animal–The Story of Freud and Tausk* (New York: Knopf, 1969).

> life from the outside, a matter of "psychology," so to speak, but rather an invasion and a definition of its spontaneous flow *in vivo*; the analyst participates actively, not just by understanding. It is therefore a purely artificial expression to speak of "determination" when it is the meaning of life in its totality that is at stake. That can be experienced only as a *unity*, and yet here it must be submitted to an incongruous method of disentanglement into a chain of component links. Each link is deprived of the claim that it is, in its vital impetus, what Nietzsche called "the whole lineage of mankind up unto itself."[3]

Not only does the contemporary patient who enters individual analysis greatly differ from that life-style and life history of, say, forty years ago, but the new patient in the contemporary group therapies discussed in this book even varies more from the patient of the past and even from lots of our patients in individual analysis.

If there is with our individual patients, especially those who have committed themselves to the long search in individual analysis, a desire for more permanent changes in their life, the new group patient is almost explosive and frantic in his search for quick solutions. It is as if he is saying, "Touch me and I will be changed," and unfortunately some of the new group therapies have led him to believe that such is within the realm of his grasp.

So the patient has been commercialized, and Phyllis Chesler gives a very vivid and perhaps true description of what we have arrived at with the new group patients:

---

[3]*The Freud Journal of Lou Andreas-Salome* (New York: Basic Books, 1964), pp. 72-73.

> Last year, I began receiving advertisements in the mail for "integrity encounter workshops" and "gut-level confrontations"—written in that cross-eyed American language, a shotgun marriage of technology and sentimentality that promises so much and costs even more. Schutz's *Joy*, a cookbook of cock-tease with a consultantship on its mind, was a best seller. College students wanted to experience their Marxism as a form of group exhilaration: they demanded "sensitivity training" and group therapy in the classroom. Businesses were sending their heart attack-prone executives to marathon retreats. Poverty boondoggle money was paying for the staffs of social action projects to encounter each other in the country. Typists and accountants were attending groups to be "scapegoated," given a "haircut," Synanon-style. Come-as-you-are pay-at-the-door groups were advertised every week in the *Voice*.[4]

I feel that the new group patient comes from various categories. There is the one patient who is looking for a shortcut (not necessarily a "haircut"!) for economic reasons (he cannot afford any long-term individual therapy, and after all what can he loose?), or he might be looking for a shortcut because of emotional reasons. It should be emphasized here that *most* patients in our society are *not analyzable* and by that I mean that they cannot fulfil the requirements of individual analysis, i.e., to commit themselves for at least two or three regular sessions a

---

[4]Phyllis Chesler, "Playing Instant Joy in the Lonely Crowd," *The Village Voice*, December 25, 1969.

week for a number of years.* They might feel that their problems need immediate solutions and they see depth-analysis as postponement. Even those patients who are seeing therapists on a once-a-week basis should realize that they are not engaged in any type of serious analysis but merely in some kind of supportive psychotherapy.

Then there are, of course, the dropouts from the long-term individual analysis. We all have seen them, they have traveled from one psychoanalyst to another for years and years and unfortunately none of them has ever told them that it might be better to stop altogether rather than continue the fruitless search. So in the end they might try a marathon or two or perhaps a sensitivity training weekend. They discover in their alienated selfs the desire to touch and are the tragic examples of so many of our lonely people in our technological, affluent society. Is it the price we have had to pay for the benefits (whatever they are) of the technological society? If so, the increase of despair and loneliness in our time has also activated the search for an answer and the need to be listened to.** Despair is often quiet, but it penetrates the person. It makes him helpless and *disconnected.*

---

*Too many analysts give their patients the *impression* that they can be helped and that analysis will work for them, but we should realize that in-depth analysis is not for the masses but for the select few, even if they come, as they do today, from the middle class.

**That the need to be listened to or to be heard transcends, of course, all class barriers, even in our technological society, proves a very moving article in *The New York Times* (April 26, 1970) entitled "For the Forgotten, a Play" which describes the experience of a couple of professional actors in staging plays in prisons with the prisoners as actors and where one prisoner says, "When I'm on that stage, however big or small my part, maybe for 10 minutes people will listen to me for the first time in my life."

It carries the first signs of a schizophrenic culture, the quiet withdrawal and the blank stare, and it communicates (at least to the therapist) that someone has given up after being abandoned himself. I have written elsewhere[5] that unless we solve the sense of despair and separateness, the fragmentation of our selves, and the lack of meaningful goals, we will face larger and more serious crises in our contemporary society, which ultimately only leads to the establishment of a totalitarian regime and society. But it should also be noted here that even the new group therapies, and the new group patients, are a part of the affluent middle class. Psychotherapy or psychoanalysis has really never reached the lower class or the ghetto.*

Another category of new group patients are those patients who were never exposed to psychotherapy, but have been attracted by the newness of it all, the desire to-be-in, "to be with it," to be able to say "I was at Esalen," to have seen the master of Esalen—Perls. Perhaps they are also a part of those who are fruitlessly seeking for quick solutions for their age-old problems. They grasp everything and anything, from astrology (the latest kick) to Eastern philosophy, they are looking for pseudo-religions, they are looking for answers which no one can give them. And they probably often do not even know the questions.

But then again should we not provide all of these categories of patients with at least the help

[5]See my books, *The Individual and the Crowd: A Study of Identity in America* (New York: Mentor Books, 1965) and *The Male Myth* (New York: Dell, 1967).

*I think that probably the social workers in this country are carrying that burden, i.e., to consult and to support the disturbed and confused members of the ghetto.

they are trying to get? I will discuss in the last chapter in more detail some of the pitfalls of the new group therapies, but I think we should realize that somehow they are meeting a need. Although by now many of the new group therapies are commercialized, it is simply the price one has to pay when such a new form of therapy emerges and is not like the individual therapy protected by a traditional structure.

There is another category of patients in the whirl of the new group therapies. A considerable number of patients who are engaged in the process of depth analysis do feel the need for some adjunct group therapy. After all they are a part of a mass society and want to test some of their own beliefs and disbeliefs in therapeutic groups. For those patients participation in an encounter group or marathon might be very enlightening and helpful. It might stimulate some of their stalled thinking and they might be able to apply some of their insights, gained in their individual analysis, in the group experience.

In a mobile, fast-changing and pressured society like ours more alternatives should be presented to those who are seeking for help and insight into their own lives. The alternative of the new group therapies is only one of them but it might be able to provide some of our troubled people with a flash of insight, a moment of truth and a moment of rest and peace.

THE NEW GROUP THERAPIST ROLE AND COMMITMENT

Those therapists who are now engaged in the conducting and business of the new group therapies bear heavy responsibilities, primarily because this is a totally new field where standards are almost unknown. Nevertheless only those therapists who have been well analyzed and trained themselves should conduct the various encounter groups and other new groups in group psychotherapy. Too many untrained people, with no diagnostic skills whatsoever, with a great many personal problems themselves, with no inkling as to what countertransference means, have entered in the field of the new group therapies and, I am sure, have been most harmful to the participants of these groups.

The issue of the responsibility and qualifications of the new group therapist cannot easily be dismissed. It can, of course, be said that qualification and training alone does not make a group therapist or, for that matter, any therapist. But the training of individual and group therapists by responsible institutes at least is a safeguard. Every therapist, be he individual or group therapist, knows how important his own countertransference feelings are in the therapeutic situation, and regardless of the claims of some of the new group therapists "that they are not doing psychotherapy," it cannot be denied that the same process of transference and countertransference enters into the therapy situation. If a therapist has not worked through, to at least a certain degree, his own problems (or at least has some cognizance of them), such a therapist is not conflict-free and hence can do the participants of the group great harm.

I am sure that many of the readers can come up with examples of miserable failures in orthodox and even in nonorthodox therapists, but that does not justify the almost total lack of training in many of the new group therapists. Attending some seminars at Esalen or a training weekend at Anthos does not make a group therapist. On the contrary it encourages the influx of amateurs and people who want to cash in on the current popularity of the new group therapies. Many of these fly-by-night therapists might think that Freud is irrelevant now, but they forget that Freud taught us many essential aspects of the therapeutic situation which are still very valid today. It is quite easy to dismiss the wisdom of the past but there seems very little to replace it with. As a matter of fact the de-emphasis in current society upon learning and the emphasis on things that are only interesting for the student has introduced a dangerous precedent in our culture. No physician can be trained in a week or two, neither can a lawyer, so I see no justification for the argument that group therapists can be trained in a very short time. Group therapy just like individual therapy requires a great deal of skill and insight on the part of the therapist. This has little to do with what school you are representing, but it has everything to do with the vast knowledge and insights a therapist is *supposed* to bring to the analytic situation. It certainly is not enough that the group therapist is an open guy and is not afraid of touching and confronting the participants. He should have also the *knowledge* as when to do it or not do it. Such an insight can *only* be required after the therapist has had sufficient training, for example, in diagnostic skills. Our society is overrun with psychotics and borderline psychotics, but can they be detected by our untrained, but smooth, group therapists? If not they invite disaster, not necessarily in the immediate group situation, but afterwards when the participant has left the group situation and is thrown back into his own world.

Bertram Forer writes about the current role of the therapist:

> With the current emphasis spotlighting the therapeutic role of the relationship between clients and therapists, the role of the therapist needs clarification. If the therapist views his rolc largely as a refined use of technical skills, he is likely to reinforce his clients' use of words as a means of hiding themselves and maintaining the status quo. To become a therapist requires a form of adaptation which *pretends* to relationships as a clever, socially rewarded method of helping others while being largely unaffected by

> them. Too often therapists use their work as a surrogate for human relationships and to avoid recognition of their own developmental failures. They can use the relationship as a means of furthering their own growth.[1]

This shows how important it is that those therapists who are conducting the encounter groups and marathons are aware of their own position and are capable of handling the various problems that the conducting of such groups produces. Arthur Burton also raises the question of training and qualification of the new group therapist:

> It is true that some encounter leaders are trained psychotherapists, but a number of them have themselves become disillusioned with psychotherapy and are hostile toward it. None of them, as far as I know, believe this to be evidence of the need for more personal analysis on their part. Others legitimately believe that the psychotherapeutic well has run dry, and that a new source of healing and growth is needed. They are looking sincerely for a new theory of man—and a concomitant practice to humanize him. Others cannot meet the professional standards of clinical practice but nevertheless feel a calling to help people. A kind of anarchy takes over in which the leader with the greatest charisma, and perhaps the most diversified "awakening" techniques, is most desired and has the greatest following. Each leader builds a personal following by collecting testimonials and quickly forgets his own obligation to science. While industry has set

---

[1]Bertram R. Forer, "Therapeutic Relationships in Groups," in *Encounter*, Arthur Burton, ed., p. 36.

> some standards for its human relation consultants, the broader exponents of encounter have not and do not promise to do so. I predict that in the decade ahead encounter leaders will require certification or licensing by the state once the evils have accumulated sufficiently to arouse public response.[2]

Once the question of training and proper qualifications has been resolved there still remains the larger question as to what kind of person the new group therapist should be. We all have the standard image of the orthodox therapist, detached and somewhat withdrawn, careful and somewhat closed off, not willing to reveal himself, and often silent and noncommunicative. Unfortunately this image has been pinned on the person of Sigmund Freud. Elsewhere[3] I have argued that no such a man ever existed and that the second generation of orthodox analysts molded Freud in their *own* image and to their own neurotic advantage. H. D. (Helen Doolittle) in her ignored little book, *Tribute to Freud** has painted a quite human and touching picture of the professor, and in a recent article, "H. D. and the 'Blameless Physician,'" Norman Holland has examined the whole relationship between H. D. as analysand

---

[2]Arthur Burton, "Encounter, Existence and Psychotherapy," *Encounter*, p. 24.

[3]See my book, *A Primer of The New Therapies*, chapter 8 (in press) and also my chapter, "Freud as Therapist" in my forthcoming book, *The Psychoanalytic Situation* (New York: Atherton Press).

*The report of H. D. on her analysis with Freud is, to be sure, an exception, as I have pointed out before. Very few written reports on the analysands of Freud are available at this point. In my forthcoming biography of Freud I have tried to assemble as many records on the encounter of some analysands with Freud.

and Freud as analyst.[4] And Norman Holmes Pearson in commenting upon Freud's relationship to H. D. said,

> . . . you do learn an enormous amount about how Freud proceeded with an analysand, how indirect Freud often was, how he seemed *not to get to the Freudian points on which Freudian critics placed such an emphasis* [author's italics]. You find two spirits responding to each other in little ways, represented not by words but by gardenias, not by poems but by friendly notes. And I can see for this particular kind of contribution why Ernest Jones, Freud's biographer, was so kind in his very brief review. "My only regret," he said, "is that I can never again read this book for the first time." He meant by that that it gave you a side of Freud which we seldom are allowed to perceive, looking always, as we are asked to do, at the grave demeanor of a man who had formulas.[5]

Probably even some of our new group therapists would benefit from the kind of relationship Freud established with H. D. Most analysts lack the relaxation and spontaneity that constitute important elements in the analytic relationship, be it group or individual therapy.

The humaneness of the group therapist has to be a foremost point in any kind of group work. He sim-

---

[4]Norman N. Holland, "H. D. and the 'Blameless Physician,'" *Contemporary Literature* (Autumn, 1969), Vol. 10, No. 4. See also his article, "Freud and H. D.," *The International Journal of Psycho-Analysis* (1969), Vol. 50. This article is also included in my forthcoming *Freud As We Knew Him* (Detroit: Wayne State University Press).

[5]"Norman Holmes Pearson on H. D.: An Interview" in *Contemporary Literature* (Autumn, 1969), Vol. 10, No. 4.

ply cannot afford to be detached but has to be *engaged* in the process of what is going on in the group at all times. This puts a rather heavy burden on him and such a task is quite taxing and emotionally straining, but I do not think it can be done otherwise.

The therapists who find group work most successful are those whose personal presentation and character structure lead them into *intense* relating with several people simultaneously. They have developed a conviction arising out of their own emotional growth efforts that most (if not, all) adults harbor a profound drive to continue growing. Effective group therapists do not expect this drive to be manifested in their patients as if by spontaneous combustion. They are prepared to employ open techniques, and perhaps more daring techniques, and to risk involving their own personalities. The effective group therapist is the first to expose himself to the mercy of the group. There may be times when the therapist sits out a delay in group participation, but more often he is likely to be ready to enliven the group experience by means of personal questions,* suggestions to participants which will relieve them of some ambivalence, or personal comments about group members. In all of this the group therapist should be careful to maintain a group focus, which means strict avoidance of his doing individual therapy on just one participant at a time. Such individual analysis in the group constitutes subgrouping, which *reduces* intense group interaction just as much as if the subgrouping were a private conversation between the therapist and a given patient.

*It has been my own personal experience as a group therapist that one works most effectively in *any kind* of group therapy when one personally commits oneself without restraints.

Certainly an important function of the group therapist is to help group members utilize the group operations with the greatest potential effectiveness. Another important function is the promotion of *risk-taking*—entering areas which seem new and dangerous for the participants. Risk-taking will most likely take place in an atmosphere of trust, and the group leader has a specific role in promoting the sense of trust, not through his bedside manner but through what he can show of himself under appropriate circumstances. People develop expectations of one another depending upon what they see, and the group therapist is no exception. Unless he shows himself, the expectations built around him will be based upon the mythology of the leader or charismatic father figure—unrealistic and unduplicatable in the world outside the group. The group therapist has the option of showing himself in how he deals with a personal crisis that arises within the group; his own honesty and strength in dealing with personal confrontation directed at him reveal a good deal of his capacity under stress.

The new group therapist can show his anxiety, his own anger and his joy at the improvement of members of the group. John Warkentin writes that, "it is an advantage to the group therapist when his anxiety and tension are readily apparent."[6]

One should also realize that for a long time therapists were not allowed to show their excitement, aliveness and enjoyment, and . . . anger. The new group encounter techniques have provided the therapist with new opportunities to use these qualities in the interest of the patient.

We should add another important aspect to the

---

[6]John Warkentin, "Intensity in Group Encounter," *Encounter,* Arthur Burton, ed.

situation of the new group therapist. It concerns the role and place of psychotherapy in our society today. Vivian Gornick in her articles on the new therapies for the *Village Voice* quotes Paul Goodman:

> Psychotherapy will become more and more pedagogic and religious. It will provide the authority of instruction and the consolation of ritual. Why even now, in places like Summerhill, the kids are being taught how to release hostility through therapeutic exercises, and at Esalen they're building a school for children. And as for religion, why, when I feel lousy, right away I do my meditating exercises . . .

Gornick continues:

> I do not agree with Mr. Goodman. That is, I do not agree that psychotherapy will successfully become instructive and spiritually healing. I *do* not believe that in this passionate displacement psychotherapy will reflect the mounting failure of our civilization, and the terrifying persistence of human hungers which a civilization must come to some terms with.

So therapists and new group therapists alike should not see themselves as the saviours or Messiahs of society, as in a sense, does Goodman. Psychotherapy does not heal and neither do the new group therapies, and it is of the utmost significance that therapists engaged in this activity will realize this. We provide insights and awareness and are not providing our patients with a way of life, but more or less prepare them for *their* encounter with life and the world. In a world like ours, which is far more complex than Freud's ever was, this does complicate the task of the therapist, but that even requires more of a thorough knowledge on the part of therapist of what moves society and the individual at this point in our civilization.

This certainly has not made the task of the new group therapist any easier, he cannot hide or avoid but is very much part of the group involvement. It requires his skill, tact and insight, but also his compassion to work within such a new group situation.

WHERE DO WE GO FROM HERE? OUTLOOKS AND CRITICISMS

Imagine a typical new group. The pressure to experience awareness is enormous, and the urge to fake it is almost irresistible. Most group members have been coached by friends and by promotional brochures: they believe that a peak experience is not only desirable but necessary, if one is to have fullest happiness and mental health. They are programmed for peaks. Further, elation or perceptual strangeness inducd by mildly hypnotic or hallucinogenic techniques can easily provide the outward and visible signs of an inner awareness.

In a society like ours, in which sensuality has long been suppressed, sensory awareness—an intense, guiltless concentration upon the sights, sounds, feels and smells of the human and natural world—can represent a revelatory experience and be almost deliriously pleasant. Unfortunately, such sensory awareness tends to occur precisely within a context that reinforces an already well-rooted reaction against mind and thought. Public education has deprived the intellectual experience of significance and emotional excitement, and intricate newfound pleasures of sensory awareness compound the tendency to regard the intellect as the great enemy of all that is natural and human and fun.

I believe that one of the greatest dangers of the new groups is its emphasis on antiintellectualization. And by that I mean that I detect a distinct antiintellectual trend among the elite of the leaders who conduct the new groups. Sure, we should not permit our patients to intellectualize their problems, but on the other hand, I feel that in the new groups too much of an emphasis is being placed on the emotions and feelings of the patients. Disregard knowledge and intellect and we end up with a society of morons. Insight is not to be divorced from knowledge and those who only depend on emotions will find themselves in the end in serious trouble.

Moreover in a society which already has deemphasized the achievements of knowledge and education and which tends to compromise ad infinitum with the nonintellectual forces in our midst, we will arrive at a culture where the blandness and dullness of its inhabitants will signify the total disintegration of personal and individual values.

The appearance of an antiintellectual trend in the new groups has not yet been recognized because too many people are still caught up in the glamour of the moment, but if there is anything that can be held against the new groups it is their lack of intellectual depth. I simply do not believe that one can treat the complexities of the human psyche in such simplistic terms as many of the new group therapies do.

So there we are; most people attending the new groups are the refugees from the middle class, and they people the workshops that dot the coast of Southern California and are scattered more sparsely elsewhere in the United States. New growth centers have proliferated. Kairos at Rancho Santa Fe, near San Diego in southernmost California, the Topanga Center for Human Development in the Los Angeles area, Shalai in Vancouver, Amare in Bowling Green, Ohio, Evergreen Institute in Littleton, Colorado and the Aureon Institute in New York City are only a few of the more than sixty centers now in existence. And what is there to come? A therapeutic community? Fritz Perls predicts such a phenomenon in his latest book,[1] but then we might have come full cycle. There should not be such a difference between a therapeutic community and a commune. Is that what this technological and de-personalized society is striving for? Are all those who are engaged in group work and/or community work trying, perhaps unconsciously, to conform to the organization, even if it is a therapeutic organization, after all?

I must admit that such a development (but where else do we go from here?) would be most disturbing for all of us. After all, we are all engaged in some form of therapy in order to free the individual patient from the bonds that prevent him from being free, open, have a sense of well being, see his place in the world, and achieve a level of happiness.

The danger of the new group therapies is perhaps also that they are being placed in contrast to

---

[1]Fritz Perls, *In and Out the Garbage Pail.*

individual therapy and that most participants simply do not realize that nothing is farther from the truth. Neither the new groups nor the traditional group therapies are or will be a replacement for individual therapy. Insights into one's own self are not achieved at easily and quickly and, moreover, insights also have to be sustained and applied. The new group therapies, as far as I can determine, do not prepare the participants for any sustaining of their newly won (and often fragile) insights, let alone that they prepare them for the application of their insights. Therefore individual therapy which works patiently with the patient to help him work on application of his insights remains a *conditio sine qua non* for the ultimate achievement of the patient in psychotherapy. Now I admit that in the experience of the new group therapies there can be a great deal of exhilaration and joy in the awareness of having discovered something new and exciting, and often that is exactly the attraction of the new group therapies. But *joy* is not the only experience we have in the world. It is probably one of the lasting contributions of the existential school of psychoanalysis that it stressed the despair and nothingness of our contemporary lives, which we simply cannot deny in the light of what takes place in our contemporary world.

That is probably one of the greatest drawbacks of the new group therapies, that they promise so much and still have produced little in terms of long-term individual growth and happiness. Follow-up reports on all the new group therapies are notoriously

---

*I wrote Dr. Perls at Esalen several times asking him for any follow-up material, but never received an answer. Dr. Elizabeth Mintz, marathon therapist in New York, provided me with an unpublished paper on the follow-up results of some

poor or not available,* but the immediate relief is there and, after all, no one really stays to tell the ultimate tale. In all the new therapeutic centers and encounter groups there is the element of temporariness. Although all of the new group therapies reject the verbiage of the old therapies, they themselves are guilty of talking endlessly about all what the participants have gained, but are rather vague about hard-core results.

There is a great deal of talk in the new group therapies about the fact that for the first time people are beginning to *feel,* that they discover how to touch and, in effect, discover their own body (and hopefully their mind). I am not too impressed with that either. The fact that people in this society are now beginning to discover the idea of touch, embracing, affection, etc., only shows how repressed society and people really are, but it does not necessarily make a case. In other societies, including the European one, the idea and practice of physical touch is quite well accepted and has been for many years. That Americans in general do equate touch with sexuality is part of the repressive culture they have been reared in for quite a number of years.

I believe that those defects (if one would label them as such) have always been with us in this society. It is only now that we cannot ignore them any longer. Essentially this has always been a *lonely society,* and consequently most people do reach for straws, even if it is only an encounter weekend. That does not make it necessarily bad, but we should be careful to hail the new group therapies as the revelation of the 1960s or, perhaps, the 1970s. They just

---

of her marathons. I must admit that her results were rather good in that most participants had tried to carry through and use the insights gained from the marathon experience.

arrived at the right moment and meant indeed a great deal for many people in terms of their personal lives and the struggles they are engaged in.

What strikes me as important is that the new group therapies refuse to a large extent to tell the patients that this world is not all made of honey and roses and that human misery is as much a part of our experience as anything else. What we try to achieve at in *any form* of therapy is that we are able to deal with this world and that, to some extent, we can function within it. For those who reject this world outright and do not wish to function in it, there are other ways of escaping this world. The drug scene and the retreat into all the pseudo-religious movements, the withdrawal into communes and other forms of separating oneself from the world, are just as many indications of how people are incapable of confronting (*not adjusting to*) the world. Paul Tillich's phrase, *The Courage To Be* is still relevant and should be taken to heart by many who try to get a fast cure out of the new group therapies. If there is anything that the new group therapies lack it is their absence of the human perspective, and W. H. Auden in writing his celebrated poem to the memory of Freud really captures this:

> He wasn't clever at all: he merely told
> the unhappy Present to recite the Past
> like a poetry lesson till sooner
> or later it faltered at the line where
> long ago the accusations had begun,
> and suddenly knew by whom it had been
>   judged,
> how rich life had been and how silly,
> and was life-forgiven and more humble,
> able to approach the Future as a friend

> without a wardrobe of excuses, without
> a set mask of rectitude or an
> embarrassing over-familiar gesture.[2]

The emphasis on the NOW by the new group therapies is certainly immensely important, but the denial of the past (since many of us have incorporated this) does not leave the patient with much. One cannot tear at the past without providing the patient with some viable alternative. "Haircuts" might be fine, but the hair will grow back and so the patient will have to face it all over again.

The new group therapies certainly have not *replaced* psychoanalysis per se (they probably never even intended to), they simply have filled a need for many people who for many complex reasons could not be reached by psychoanalysis or psychotherapy. A substitute? Well at best a poor one. Psychoanalysis is still the best available tool we have at this moment for the individual to work in depth on the problems that he is confronting in his life and in the world.

Ronald Laing once wrote that psychoanalysis is essentially a *re-search:*

> The psychotherapeutic relationship is therefore a re-search. A search, constantly reasserted and reconstituted, for what we have all lost and whose loss some can perhaps endure a little more easily than others, and *this re-search is validated by the shared experience of experience regained in and through the therapeutic relationship in the here and now.*[3]

---

[2]W. H. Auden, "In Memory of Sigmund Freud" *Collected Shorter Poems, 1927–1957* (London: Faber & Faber, 1966), p. 167.

[3]R. D. Laing, *The Politics of Experience* (New York, Pantheon Books, 1967), p. 34.

Research does take time and reflection. The shortcuts provided by the new group therapies are there (and for many fortunately so), but in the long run: How long do they last?